THE 1968 PROJECT

A NATION COMING OF AGE

THE 1968 PROJECT

A NATION COMING OF AGE

INTRODUCTION BY
Brian Horrigan

EPILOGUE BY
Brad Zellar

COMPILED BY
Elizabeth Ault

WITH CONTRIBUTIONS BY
Brad Zellar
Brian Horrigan
Elizabeth Ault
and the Minnesota Historical Society staff

Minnesota Historical
Society Press

An extraordinary year. An unforgettable experience. The year 1968 comes alive with immersive environments, artifacts, and interactives in The 1968 Exhibit, which kicks off its national tour at the Minnesota History Center. www.the1968exhibit.org

The 1968 Exhibit has been made possible in part by major grants from the National Endowment for the Humanities: Because democracy demands wisdom.

The 1968 Exhibit has also been supported by a "Museums for America" grant from the Institute of Museum and Library Services (IMLS), the primary source of federal support for the nation's 123,000 libraries and 17,500 museums.

Photograph and illustration credits for the book are given on p. 167.

www.mhspress.org

The Minnesota Historical Society Press is a member of the Association of American University Presses.

Book design by Percolator Graphic Design, Minneapolis

Manufactured in the United States of America

10 9 8 7 6 5 4 3 2 1

♾ The paper used in this publication meets the minimum requirements of the American National Standard for Information Sciences—Permanence for Printed Library Materials, ANSI Z39.48–1984.

International Standard Book Number
ISBN: 978-0-87351-842-0

Library of Congress Cataloging-in-Publication Data

The 1968 project : a nation coming of age / introduction by Brian Horrigan ; epilogue by Brad Zellar ; compiled by Elizabeth Ault ; with contributions by Brad Zellar, Brian Horrigan, Elizabeth Ault, and the Minnesota Historical Society staff.
 p. cm.
 The 1968 Project is the accompanying book to The 1968 Exhibit, a major traveling exhibition developed by the Minnesota Historical Society, in partnership with the Atlanta History Center, the Chicago History Museum, and the Oakland Museum of California.
 Includes bibliographical references and index.
 ISBN 978-0-87351-842-0 (pbk. : alk. paper)
 1. United States—History—1961–1969—Exhibitions. 2. United States—Social conditions—1960–1980—Exhibitions. 3. Nineteen sixty-eight, A.D.—Exhibitions. 4. Social movements—United States—History—20th century—Exhibitions. 5. Counterculture—United States—History—20th century—Exhibitions. 6. Popular culture—United States—History—20th century—Exhibitions. 7. Documentary photography—United States—Exhibitions. I. Zellar, Brad. II. Horrigan, Brian. III. Ault, Elizabeth. IV. Minnesota Historical Society. V. Title: Nineteen sixty-eight project.
 E846.A189
 973.923—dc23
 2011036298

CONTENTS

INTRODUCTION

Brian Horrigan

WHEN DID 1968 become "1968"? When did that single year come to stand in for everything that was wrong and everything that was right about the sixties? When did it become the year that rocked the world, the year everything changed, the year that made us who we are?

Other eventful years in the 1960s could collect their share of votes in a straw poll for most earth-shattering: 1967 was the year of the Six-Day War, the Summer of Love, and antiwar demonstrations at the Pentagon; or 1969, the year of the moon landing and the Manson murders, the year of Woodstock, Stonewall, and Chappaquiddick. But 1968 continues to resonate most forcefully in American memory for the relentless concatenation of events rolling off the year's calendar, for the feeling, as more than one observer has remembered it, of "one damn thing after another."

It is certainly debatable whether any single year can be thought of as pivotal in a fluid era when so many aspects of society appeared to be in flux. Yet even in 1968 there seemed to be a broad awareness that the year was not only momentous but transformational. One gets an impression of an entire world left spent and shaken as the year finally shuddered to an end in December.

Retrospectives began immediately: *Life* magazine devoted an entire issue in January 1969 to an exhausting pictorial survey of what it called "that incredible year." The year brought the Tet Offensive in Vietnam and the highest yearly death toll of American soldiers in the conflict's long history. Massive waves of young people surged into the streets and onto the campaign trail for antiwar candidate Eugene McCarthy. The year saw the assassinations of Martin Luther King Jr. and Robert Kennedy, a poor people's Resurrection City built on the National Mall, and riots at the Democratic party convention. There were assertions of Black Power at the Olympic Games and women's liberation at the Miss America pageant. *Hair* opened on Broadway, *Laugh-In* debuted on television, Johnny Cash gave a legendary performance at Folsom Prison, and Aretha Franklin shouted at us to "Think!" The Beatles had their greatest year ever, and Elvis made a comeback.

The year witnessed a conservative political resurgence with the rise of George Wallace and Ronald Reagan. President Lyndon Johnson spoke in his 1968 State of the Union address of a country "challenged at home and abroad," of an uneasy "restlessness" among the American people. Richard Nixon, in his speech accepting his party's nomination for president, said that we "live in an age of revolution," that "historians will recall that 1968 marked the beginning of the American generation in world history. Just to be alive at this time is an experience unparalleled in history." In the closing days of the year, the planet Earth became visible in its entirety for the first time, a slowly turning point of light, seen from the window of the *Apollo 8* space capsule.

In 2008 I became part of a team charged with developing a major traveling exhibition on the year 1968, in partnership with museums in Atlanta, Chicago, and Oakland. For me, the project hit close to home, more than any other in my thirty-year career developing history exhibits. 1968 was the year I turned eighteen, graduated from high school, and headed off to college. It was my year of personal transformation, of reshaping identity, of virtually catapulting from one place and one state of mind to another. Looking back on that trajectory—as I inevitably did while researching this book and the 1968 exhibit—I realize how closely my experience mirrored that of millions of other young people that year.

I lived a fairly sheltered life in Houston, Texas, in Middle America (although we didn't call it that then). I came from a working-class family and had a straitlaced Catholic education. My parents were members of what came to be known as the Greatest Generation, both born in the Midwest. Dad was a Republican (he voted for Nixon five times in national elections), and my mother was a Kennedy Democrat and a stay-at-home, car-pooling mom. The house had air-conditioners and televisions, and there were two cars in the driveway. I can barely recall thinking about the war in Vietnam 1968, except when a high school classmate's brother was killed there, and he got a full-page memorial in our yearbook.

When I heard the news of Dr. King's assassination I was at choir practice, where we were rehearsing our fresh-faced rendition of "Up with People." All I recall about Bobby Kennedy's death in early June was that some people in my class were upset because it cast a pall over our senior prom. When we graduated, the senior class sang, en masse and without embarrassment (then, at least) "The Impossible Dream." I worked my last summer in Houston at a shiny new amusement park, and I was as clean-cut a teenager as you can imagine. I can't recall hearing about or even thinking much about the violence during the Democratic National Convention, an ignorance all the more strange since that's where I was headed—Chicago—in just a few weeks to start my first year of college.

And so I got onto a jet plane in September 1968. Like millions of other people that year, when magazine articles were warning about backed-up runways and crowded skies, I was taking my first trip on a plane. And so on to Chicago: bustling, dirty, dangerous, exciting, exhilarating. A place to wake up and discover the rest of the world of 1968. By the time the next year rolled around my hair was long, a shaggy beard was growing in, and the black horn-rimmed glasses were replaced by wire rims. I acquired peasant shirts, Jesus sandals, a beaded necklace, a taste for cheap wine and marijuana, and quite a few new vocabulary words. I stopped going to church and decided I was an atheist. I went to teach-ins on campus about the war, supported a sit-in at the university (though I personally sat out), helped a friend connect with an underground abortion clinic, and marched in massive antiwar demonstrations downtown. I left the unremarkable first half of my 1968 far behind, along with large parts of my old self, and tried on some new things.

Developing an exhibit and producing a book on a single year, especially one as transformative as 1968, presented significant challenges. The familiarity of so much of the material—at least to visitors and readers within a certain age group—is a two-edged sword. On the one hand, many people have immense personal caches of knowledge about the era. But along with that comes the potential for biases and prejudices and settled opinions.

Confining a project to a single year is only theoretically limiting. In practice there are an infinite number of stories to tell and choices to make. So many of the events of the year are so historically critical that it would be impossible to leave any one of them out. This could easily lead to a greatest-hits approach. We also wanted to pay due respect to the familiar, the essential, while leaving room for the quirky and unexpected, to remember that a year has a kind of continuous fabric, that it's not always about the rips and the explosions. We wanted to represent the year as a whole, with all of its complexities and contradictions and contested memories.

Race, violence, liberation, power: all of these and other large themes course through both the exhibit and this book. But there is also a kaleidoscoping sense of overlapping, sometimes incongruous coincidences. Disparate events—the massacre of protesters at Orangeburg State College in February, for example, on the day the Olympic Winter Games opened in Grenoble; or the premiere of *2001: A Space Odyssey* on the same weekend as the King assassination and funeral; or Robert Kennedy announcing his candidacy for president on the same day that, a world away, villagers in My Lai were being massacred.

In spite of the enormous numbers of popular and scholarly studies of the year and the era it represents, there is still nothing approaching consensus on its meaning. According to Gerard DeGroot's 2008 *The Sixties Unplugged: A Kaleidoscopic History of a Disorderly Decade,* the "decade has been transformed into a morality play, an explanation of how the world went astray or, conversely, how hope was squandered. Problems of the present are blamed on myths of the past." It is the very contentiousness about this year and this decade, the manifestly unsettled nature of the historical and popular debate about meaning, about damage done or victories won, that makes this project so compelling and urgent. 1968 is everywhere around us—in our politics, our popular culture, and our national subconscious—but few of us have been able to step back and put the year into focus.

SO WHAT IS BEFORE YOU—in both this book and The 1968 Exhibit is not a wholly finished work but a work in progress, much like the contested and unsettled assessment, both scholarly and popular, of the sixties themselves. 1968 is not a lens through which to see the 1960s, since a lens implies something that pulls a wide frame into a single, crisp focus. Nor is it a snapshot, which would imply a neat, white-bordered square. Rather, 1968 is seen as prismatic, a year that gathers in all the blinding light of the era, fracturing it and shattering it into its many contentious parts.

Gathering all those shards of light into a book and an exhibit has been challenging, to say the least. But looking back on 1968, both as a year and as a symbol, I find myself returning again and again to some of the year's most salient themes.

THE WHOLE WORLD IS WATCHING

The year 1968 stands out for the truly global character of the political upheaval and social turbulence. Protesters at the Democratic National Convention in Chicago in August 1968 chanted "the whole world is watching," and they were right. Not only was the whole world watching what was going on in the United States and Vietnam, but the converse was also true: Americans were witness to political protest, challenges to authority, and violent repression not only in European capitals but also in Algeria, Senegal, Japan, China, and Brazil. Students and trade-unionist work-ers clashed with police on barricaded Paris streets in May 1968. In October in Mexico City, just days before the start of the Olympic Games, government forces brutally attacked student protesters. Soviet tanks were rolling into Prague to suppress the Czech liberaliza-tion known as the Prague Spring on the same sweltering August days that Chicago police were erupting into violent counterattacks on antiwar protesters.

The mobilization of Soviet tanks against a westernizing state was a reminder that there was still a very frigid Cold War going on in 1968, a fact that's easy to forget in today's post-Soviet world. The Berlin Wall had been constructed just seven years earlier; China, still referred to as Red China, was constantly saber rattling in Asia; North Korean forces captured and held hostage the crew of an American gunship for nearly all twelve months of 1968; and, although the United States and the U.S.S.R signed the Nuclear Non-Proliferation Pact that year, France con-ducted its first test of a thermonuclear device.

BODIES OF MEANING

The sixties—and even more sharply, the year 1968—witnessed a major shift in the under-standing and representation of the human body in art, culture, science, and medicine—indeed, throughout the entire public sphere. At the heart of any historical examination of American life in the 1960s is the engulf-ing tragedy of the Vietnam War. In ways, its impact on Americans was akin to that of the Civil War, with its unprecedented carnage. Americans in the 1960s were subjected to a constant, numbing visual parade of soldiers' dead bodies—every week in *Life,* every night on the TV news. The American death toll in Vietnam reached shocking levels in 1968—as many as five hundred killed in a single week in February of that year.

At the same time, Americans at home began to see more images of dead bodies of Vietnamese civilians, especially children, in antiwar posters and advertisements. The 1968 massacre at My Lai was revealed in 1969, with searing images of piled-up bodies. And in the American media there were still other disturbing images of suffering and the human body: bloated bellies of starving children, the iconic image of Biafra in mid-1968; black Americans attacked by police during the massive riots between 1966 and 1968; the very publicly murdered bodies of King and Kennedy; the flailing, bullet-riddled bodies at the gruesome climax of *Bonnie and Clyde,* one of the top films of 1968. Less violent—but to some people equally shocking—was the rise in displays of nudity, in films like *I Am Curious (Yellow),* in theaters (*Hair* and *Oh! Calcutta*), and in public at be-ins and rock festivals.

IT'S HAPPENING RIGHT NOW

Part of what gave 1968 its quicksilver character was the extent to which the entire country could experience incendiary events instantly. Through television, Americans felt the immediate impact of events that were sometimes worlds away, converting these moments into shared experiences. The most-watched television broadcast in history up to that time was the Christmas Eve relay from the *Apollo 8* crew, sending back images of the moon and the earth as they read from the book of Genesis. Sometimes events merely *seemed* to be happening in the moment: the notorious nighttime riot scenes in Chicago's Grant Park were filmed earlier but broadcast by some television networks on split screens along with actual-time convention proceedings, creating a false sense of simultaneity and heightening the outrage. But although the mass media made events seem universally accessible, at the same time, it could also mark another dividing line between Americans. The music one liked, the movies one attended, and the shows one watched signaled one's generational, political, and cultural allegiances.

LOOKING FOR WHO WE ARE

In the Cold War era of the 1950s and 1960s, Americans' search for a satisfying identity became more self-conscious than ever before. In the late 1960s, the quest for an authentic identity took on a new, socially relevant, and culturally fertile meaning. Feminist. Hippie. Student. Middle American. Black. Chicano. These and many other labels were borne proudly. As never before, the public square became an arena of contention among these identity groups, each competing with the others for space and power. The 1960s marked a watershed in American cultural history, a time when Americans embraced the idea that a clearly delineated self-concept was a requisite for a successful life.

The urgency of defining personal identity had an even larger dimension, however, in the 1960s, as developments in both technology and culture began to raise fundamental questions about life itself: What does it mean to be human? When does life begin? How will science transform the way we look, the way we behave, who we are? Breakthroughs in medicine—psychotropic drugs, heart transplants, bone-marrow transplants, *in situ* photographs of fetuses—were widely heralded in the media and led to ecstatic predictions of an unimpeded technological transformation of the human body. Novelists and filmmakers explored the possibility of manufactured humanity (Philip Dick's 1968 novel *Do Androids Dream of Electric Sheep?*); humans thrust into reversals with animals (*Planet of the Apes*); or humans transformed into monsters (*Night of the Living Dead*). Stanford scientist Paul Ehrlich's bestselling *The Population Bomb* fueled apocalyptic anxieties about an oversupply of humans using up limited resources. At the same time, Pope Paul VI issued *Humanae Vitae* (On Human Life), the Catholic Church's firmest opposition to contemporary methods of birth control—a direct challenge to those, like Ehrlich, who were eager to apply all of the powers of modern science to controlling the unchecked expansion of the human race.

CHOOSING SIDES

Less than five months into 1968, *Life* magazine could observe, "In the argot of the times the word is confrontation . . . Blacks and whites, blacks and blacks, whites and whites; students and administrators, students and students, teachers and administrators; the have-nots confront the haves; doves and hawks, ministers and bishops, marchers and countermarchers, radicals and loyalists, Americans." For an era that is often remembered as being open, freewheeling, expansive, a time in which we were repeatedly encouraged to "do your own thing," the sixties can also be seen as an era of intense polarization, often represented by simplistic dualities. Many Americans, rather than feeling encouraged to choose from a spectrum of possibilities, instead found themselves confronted with a series of stark, divisive choices: freedom versus order, change versus continuity, revolution versus reaction.

Americans had to find a way to grapple with this polarizing public culture. All around the country, bumper stickers announced, "America: Love It or Leave It" and "My Country: Right or Wrong." It was during the sharply divided 1960s that the terms "hawk" and "dove" became shorthand for political positions on the war. By the late 1960s, popular culture was dividing women into followers of traditional roles or advocates of women's liberation, a dichotomy (false though it might have been) that was sharply drawn at the first-ever protests at the Miss America pageant in September 1968.

In black America, the choice sharpened between the nonviolent civil disobedience identified with Martin Luther King Jr. and the militant tactics of the Black Power movement. Even in popular culture, there were sharp dividing lines: I remember that, in my high school, you could be either an Elvis fan or a Beatles fan, but you couldn't be both. The very premise of movies like *In the Heat of the Night* (the Oscar winner for best picture in 1968) or *Guess Who's Coming to Dinner* was the nearly unbridgeable divide between black and white Americans (though of course, since this was Hollywood, unanimity was discovered by the end). Navigating these polarities challenged every American in 1968.

YOU ARE WHAT YOU BUY

Probably no concept is more identified with the 1960s than that of the counterculture. As both a concept and a set of behaviors, the counterculture operated along an extraordinarily wide spectrum—experimentation with drugs, political protest, Black Power, Eastern philosophies, sexual liberation, back-to-the-land movements. One's allegiance was signaled by what one ate, drank, wore, bought, or drove. At the counterculture's heart, however, was a renegotiation of identity, a struggling toward defining one's place in the world that informed politics as well as culture.

On the other hand, historians have long noted the co-optation (another 1960s word) of at least the superficial symbols of the counterculture, the appropriation by corporate marketers of images, attitudes, and actual things once considered transgressive or revolutionary. Though they fundamentally disagreed about the role of material culture and advertising and consumerism, ad men and members of the counterculture agreed that consumer choices revealed something about the chooser. Thus, objects and images such as album covers, drug paraphernalia, clothing, even food and drink products can be interpreted on a wide spectrum of meaning.

It remains true, of course, that for many people, 1968 may *not* have felt like the year that everything changed. Its saturated colors and dramatic events can easily blind one to the simple fact that the year was characterized as much by continuities with the prosperous and conservative postwar years as it was with revolutionary change. After all, it was Richard Nixon—an Eisenhower-era stalwart—who won the election. And throughout popular culture that year there was ample evidence that the times were *not* changing: *2001: A Space Odyssey* may have been the seminal movie of the moment, but the most successful movie that year was a big-budget Broadway musical, *Funny Girl.* On television, *Rowan and Martin's Laugh-In* was Nielsen's top-rated show, but close behind were *Gunsmoke* and *Gomer Pyle, U.S.M.C.* And though the Beatles had the number-one record ("Hey, Jude") that year, the supposedly signature sounds of the sixties—Joplin, Hendrix, Cream, the Grateful Dead—were nowhere near the top of the record-sales lists.

NEVER TRUST ANYONE OVER THIRTY

It was the upheavals of the 1960s that gave rise to the term (if not the actual phenomenon, which had been around for centuries) "generation gap." Sociologist Kenneth Keniston, in his influential 1968 study *Young Radicals: Notes on Committed Youth,* found his informants to be "hostile . . . to patterns of power and authority." Classically, of course, young people define themselves in relation to—if not always in opposition to—the values of their parents' generation. But the 1960s sharpened this process, compelling one to find a place on one side or the other of a yawning chasm. The very concept of generations and intergenerational conflicts, real and imagined, underscored the 1960s.

While the seeds of the events of 1968 were certainly sown in the years before, after 1968 things were different, particularly for America's young people: the Baby Boom generation. Today, those Americans who were coming of age in the 1960s—serving in Vietnam, burning draft cards, getting "clean for Gene," or carrying the conservative banner of the Young Americans for Freedom—are now on their way to becoming our nation's elders. They have raised families, established careers, nurtured the economy, and participated in the country's political, social, and cultural evolution, and they have begun to pass the reins of power to a generation too young to remember 1968.

The events of 1968 catalyzed a persistent, if often contradictory, sense of identity for this generation. As historian Mike Wallace—a graduate student at Columbia University in 1968 during the student protests there—recollected in an oral history interview,

> I was in the midst of an enormous tide of people . . . The ecstasy was stepping out of time, out of traditional personal time. It was phenomenally liberating. At the same time it was a political struggle. And it wasn't just Columbia. There *was* a war on in Vietnam, and the civil rights movement. These were profound forces that transcend that moment. 1968 just cracked the universe open for me.

Publisher's Note

The Minnesota Historical Society staff, both from the MHS Press and the MHS exhibits team, as well as writer Brad Zellar contributed essays to *The 1968 Project*. All essays have been identified with the writers' initials, and the contributors' biographies are listed at the back of the book.

JANUARY The Living Room War

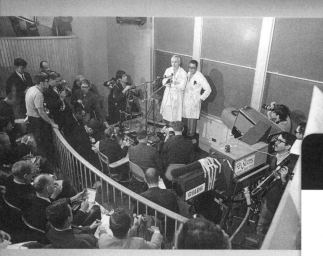

Saturday 13
JANUARY

Backed by June Carter, Carl Perkins, and the Tennessee Three, Johnny Cash performs two shows at Folsom State Prison in California, revitalizing a career stunted by drug abuse and limited commercial success.

Saturday 6
JANUARY

The first adult human-to-human heart transplant operation in the United States is performed at Stanford University Medical Center in California.

Sunday 14
JANUARY

The Green Bay Packers defeat the Oakland Raiders in the second AFL-NFL World Championship Game—later to be known as the Super Bowl— at the Orange Bowl in Miami.

Monday 15
JANUARY

A group of women's peace organizations join together to confront Congress on its opening day with a display of opposition to the Vietnam War. At age 87, pioneering suffragist Jeannette Rankin leads the march of approximately 5,000 women.

Wednesday 17
JANUARY

Lyndon Baines Johnson delivers his State of the Union address, stating that in Vietnam "the enemy has been defeated in battle after battle" and that "our patience and our perseverance will match our power."

Thursday 18
JANUARY

Singer and actress Eartha Kitt denounces the Vietnam War to Lady Bird Johnson while attending a White House luncheon meeting focusing on crime and juvenile delinquency.

Sunday 21
JANUARY

A U.S. Air Force B-52 carrying four hydrogen bombs crashes into sea ice near Thule Air Base in Greenland, spreading radioactive contamination over a large area and ratcheting up Cold War tensions.

Monday 22
JANUARY

Rowan and Martin's Laugh-In airs for the first time on NBC. With its rapid-fire sexually and politically charged gags and sketches, it becomes the Nielsen ratings' number-one show by the start of the fall TV season.

Tuesday 23
JANUARY

A North Korean patrol boat captures the USS *Pueblo*, an intelligence-gathering vessel. One American serviceman is killed and the rest of the crew of 82 are taken hostage, accused by North Korea of espionage and violating territorial waters. The crew will not be released for nearly a year.

Wednesday 31
JANUARY

Shortly after midnight North Vietnamese forces begin the massive assault on South Vietnam known as the Tet Offensive. The North Vietnamese wage war up and down the country, taking the war to the heart of Saigon and attacking the new American embassy compound.

"This situation is getting more serious with Communist attacks against seven province capitals in central Vietnam and the highlands on the very night of the New Year [Tet] . . . I declare the state of martial law throughout the nation from today until further notice." —NGUYEN VAN THIEU, PRESIDENT OF SOUTH VIETNAM, JANUARY 31, 1968

AS THE YEAR 1968 OPENED, the mood of the country was fearful and nervous, with Americans looking warily to another year of violence and turmoil. The most immediate concern was the deteriorating state of race relations. The goodwill generated by Lyndon Johnson's Great Society initiatives and the Voting Rights Act of 1965 was being violently erased by explosive conflicts in inner cities and by a steadily rising crime rate. On January 26 the editors of *Time* magazine wrote, "Now, after four summers of holocausts in the nation's largest cities, concern over the Negro's welfare has been largely replaced by consternation at the prospect of anarchy." By 1968 the word "summer" was conjuring not only beaches and vacations and reruns on TV, but also the looted, burned-out wreckage of America's urban cores.

The nation's increasingly deadly military involvement in Vietnam was steadily escalating, but in the month before the Tet Offensive, news from Vietnam often failed to make the front pages of newspapers, and it was even possible, in the middle of January, for *Life* magazine to publish an entire issue without mentioning the war. Americans at home were still able to focus their attention elsewhere— on the wacky new TV show *Laugh-In* that debuted that month; the Winter Olympics, soon to open in Grenoble, France; or Hollywood's breakout hits *Bonnie and Clyde* and *The Graduate,* both soaring at the box office.

In January of an election year, the political focus was turning to the upcoming primaries. Upstart Democrat Eugene McCarthy would make headlines in March by almost defeating President Johnson for his party's nomination. But as the year opened, all of the political jockeying was happening on the Republican side. Former vice president Richard Nixon was already considered the front-runner, though he didn't announce his candidacy until February 1. Michigan governor George Romney was expected to be his closest rival, followed by longtime New York governor Nelson Rockefeller and by Ronald Reagan, who had been installed as California's governor barely a year earlier.

Besides the upcoming election, the big news in January 1968 was—according to *Newsweek* magazine—"the mighty U.S. economy, churning into its eighth straight year of unbroken prosperity." The year's horrors and turbulence, the inequalities and violence, occurred against a backdrop of increasing affluence for vast numbers of Americans. Unemployment was at less than 4 percent, and wages were on the rise. Economists in 1968 were predicting "another flood of riches from the cornucopia."

In his January 17 State of the Union address President Johnson reminded his vast national audience of the country's booming economy, sounding a note of conspicuous consumption:

> "Americans are prosperous as men have never been in recorded history . . . All about them, most American families can see the evidence of growing abundance: higher paychecks, humming factories, new cars moving

down new highways. More and more families own their own homes, equipped with more than 70 million television sets."

And yet, as he said, perceptively, "There is in the land a certain restlessness—a questioning" that "our ship is moving through new and troubled waters." No one, not even the president, could know just how prescient the opening line of his address would prove to be in the coming months: "I report to you that our country is challenged, at home and abroad." —B.H.

The affluence of the 1960s supported the development of largely white suburbs.

BLACK POWER, BLACK CROSSOVER

Black Power, black voices, and black entertainers were making unprecedented inroads in politics, television, music, film, and mainstream culture even as major newspapers, magazines, and television news programs fretted about racial violence and asked repeatedly, what does the Negro want? Aretha Franklin appeared on the covers of major magazines and the stable of artists at Detroit's Motown Re- cords—the label that had, arguably, first stumbled upon an elegant crossover formula—was turning out hit after hit that connected with white and black audiences alike and landed performers like Diana Ross and the Supremes on major television programs and radio stations all over the country.

Even the rawer and more uncompromising artists at soul labels like Atlantic and King—James

Brown, Wilson Pickett, William Bell, Booker T. and the M.G.'s, and scores of others—were making a splash both on college campuses and in the inner cities. *Billboard* magazine's 1968 artist of the year, Jimi Hendrix, was playing major festivals and covering Bob Dylan while he revolutionized rock guitar, channeling his blues forbears and milking the instrument's sonic possibilities.

Sidney Poitier starred in two of the biggest box office and critical hits of the year, *Guess Who's Coming to Dinner* and *In the Heat of the Night*. Comedians like Bill Cosby and Flip Wilson and Pigmeat Markham were staples of network television. Model Naomi Sims was a magazine cover girl and Leontyne Price was singing on the stage of the Metropolitan Opera. Yet the major media outlets of the time contained very little advertising aimed at blacks, and where any at all existed (outside of the black press), it was strictly segregated and often offensively stereotypical.

Ironically, the most fully integrated institution of the contentious year was the military, where blacks were represented in larger numbers than in the general population. Blacks were not simply a minority in the United States in 1968, they were a small minority—only 11 percent of the population. Opportunities for advancement were bleak in the inner cities and the South, where black voting power and voting rights were constantly undermined by prejudice and firmly entrenched notions about race and integration.

That black Americans were able to marshal movements on so many fronts—and attract growing attention and support from white media and politicians—is a testament to their organization, perseverance, and passion. Their appeals were increasingly embraced by their white fellow citizens as ethical common sense.

From the vantage of the twenty-first century it seems incredible that in 1968 anyone would have been debating the question, What does the Negro want? Never mind that by then the word "Negro" was already being supplanted by "black" in the popular consciousness. That the question was being asked at all reflects the general acceptance of status quo racism even in bastions of relatively well-meaning and progressive-thinking people. It also speaks to the hard-headed stubbornness with which much of the populace still clung to that status quo as a necessary American reality.

Meanwhile the explosive new medium of television was reducing politics and war and other unpleasant social realities to a bewildering spectator sport for a huge swath of the populace. As the year drew on, civil rights demonstrations were often upstaged by the war in Vietnam and unrest on campuses. Most white middle-class Americans weren't much invested in what blacks wanted anyway. The first generation to send its children off to college in huge numbers now found itself wrestling with a question of much greater personal significance: What do our children want? —B.Z.

THE MASS MEDIA BROUGHT increasingly violent images of war and political unrest into American homes as the year went on. Americans tried to process the massive flow of information they received from officials who reassured them about how well the war was going while simultaneously providing horrifying body counts. The war was brought home in other ways as well, through local or family casualties and, for millions of young men, the looming specter of the draft. A Gallup poll revealed that while a majority of Americans still preferred to describe themselves as hawks (rather than doves), only 35 percent of them approved of President Johnson's handling of the war. Regardless of anyone's position, there was a growing consensus that *something* was amiss in American life. What that thing was, and how to go about fixing it, would preoccupy the nation for the rest of the year.

"My opposition to the Vietnam War came at least in part because I was eligible for the draft."
—CHARLES BRANHAM, HISTORIAN, ORAL HISTORY INTERVIEW

LEFT: Antiwar protests mounted throughout the sixties; in 1967 an estimated 100,000 people marched on the Pentagon, where they were violently forced back. ABOVE: Tear gas and mace were frequently used by law enforcement to disperse protesters, as seen here on Madison, Wisconsin's Bascom Hill.

"I'm of two minds about the draft—I mean, I'd hate to have my kids drafted to fight a war I thought was wrong. If we were to invade Toronto tomorrow, I'd say, 'Let's not do it. Don't go. Do whatever you have to do.' On the other hand, part of me also thinks, you know, that's really what began the end of our involvement in Vietnam, that families across the country didn't think it was worth the price of their sons and daughters. But if your son or daughter is not going to be killed or wounded, you tend to forget about it, and turn to what's for dinner tonight, pork chops or chicken?" —TIM O'BRIEN, NOVELIST, ORAL HISTORY INTERVIEW

Burning one's draft card was a widespread image of resistance to the draft; this draft card was issued to a Minnesota man in 1965 (name deleted for privacy).

HELL, NO WE WON'T GO!
What about your son?

"Middle America, if you're going to vote for wars by electing the people you do, then you're going to have to pay the price. Your sons and daughters should be over there doing the killing and the dying. Otherwise don't vote. Stay out of the ballot box. And if you do vote for war, for people who bring us wars and are in favor of a war, then you have to go yourself—or your daughter or your son has to go." —TIM O'BRIEN, ORAL HISTORY INTERVIEW

LEFT: This poster riffed on a popular slogan chanted by anti-draft protesters. BELOW: Secretary of defense Robert S. McNamara, pictured here, right, with President Johnson, was known as the architect of the Vietnam War. He stepped down in February 1968.

THE POLITICS OF PRIVILEGE

Students for a Democratic Society (SDS) was founded at the University of Michigan in 1962. By 1968, with more students in college than ever before, the organization seemed newly relevant. Many students felt a growing resistance to the war for reasons both personal and ideological. Campus protests grew in number and intensity, and clashes with police became increasingly common. The visible, vocal presence of antiwar protesters played a crucial role in turning public opinion against the war—although they sometimes managed to turn public opinion against themselves as well.

Many of the student protesters were in a position of privilege simply because their status as students allowed them to avoid the draft. Both male and female students protested, but the movements were almost entirely run by men, partly because only men were eligible for the draft and partly because male dominance was ingrained in the culture. In the words of Grace LeClair, "The antiwar movement was structured the same way as everything else, in that men were the important people and women were supposed to mimeograph things and be quiet in the meetings." Political activism became a way to create new versions of masculinity that were different from inherited ones in some respects—certainly they were less authoritarian, less based on economic accumulation—but which did not shed all traditional values. The war in Vietnam gave students a common cause, but the movements they built replicated in many ways the society they came to protest. —E.A.

"The North Vietnamese and the Vietcong are not going to change their attitude by virtue of the U.S. protesting for peace . . . The only effective way . . . is to prosecute the war more effectively." —RICHARD M. NIXON, FEBRUARY 5, 1968

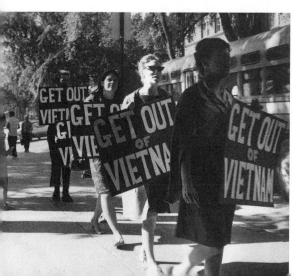

LEFT: Not all protests were confrontational; many demonstrations were everyday activities, like this one in Madison, Wisconsin. RIGHT: This poster was specifically cited by many women's liberation advocates as a catalyst for their growing feminist consciousness.

FEBRUARY

We're Losing This War

Thursday 1
FEBRUARY

Associated Press photographer Eddie Adams captures the summary execution of a Viet Cong prisoner on the streets of Saigon.

Thursday 8
FEBRUARY

In Orangeburg, South Carolina, highway patrolmen fire into a crowd of African American students protesting segregation at a local bowling alley. Three young men are killed.

•

Former Alabama governor and committed segregationist George Wallace announces his candidacy for U.S. president on the American Independent Party ticket.

Saturday 10
FEBRUARY

Nineteen-year-old Peggy Fleming captures the gold medal in women's figure skating at the Winter Olympics in Grenoble, France—the only American gold of the games.

Monday 12
FEBRUARY

The Black Panther Party's minister of information, Eldridge Cleaver, publishes *Soul on Ice*, written while he was in prison.

Friday 16
FEBRUARY

"911" emergency phone service begins with a phone call in Haleyville, Alabama.

Monday 19
FEBRUARY

The children's television program *Mister Rogers' Neighborhood*, originating at WQED-TV in Pittsburgh, is broadcast nationally for the first time.

Thursday 22
FEBRUARY

The counterculture film *Easy Rider* begins production and is substantially complete by the summer. The film will not be released until 1969, partly due to a drawn-out dispute about the length of the final edit. Dennis Hopper's first cut came in at 220 minutes.

Tuesday 27
FEBRUARY

In a nationally televised news special, CBS anchorman Walter Cronkite predicts that "the bloody experience of Vietnam" will "end in a stalemate."

Thursday 29
FEBRUARY

The Kerner Commission issues its report on the racial violence that erupted in summer 1967.

"Our Nation is moving toward two societies, one black, one white—separate and unequal." —KERNER COMMISSION REPORT, 1968

"Through careful exploitation of the enemy's vulnerabilities and application of our superior firepower and mobility we should expect our gains of 1967 to be increased manifold in 1968 . . . Our forces have been able to detect impending major offensives and to mount spoiling attacks."

—GEN. WILLIAM C. WESTMORELAND, JANUARY 1, 1968

"In my opinion this [the Tet Offensive] is a diversionary effort to take attention away from the northern part of the country."

—GEN. WESTMORELAND, FEBRUARY 1, 1968

ABOVE: Uniform helmet worn in Vietnam by a member of C Company, 508th Infantry, 82nd Airborne Division, 1968–69. RIGHT: Fatigue jacket worn in Vietnam by a member of the 101st Airborne, 47th Division.

Despite attempts to spin the response differently, by July the House Appropriations Subcommittee had concluded that "it did not dawn on our top leaders that the Tet Offensive was going to happen when it did." —JAMIE L. WHITTEN, MEMBER OF THE HOUSE APPROPRIATIONS SUBCOMMITTEE, JULY 9, 1968

"I WAS STILL GOING TO EMORY and got my 1-A card: Student deferments were gone. In the lottery I think I was 39. Luckily, I got out of it. It came time for me to go for a physical so I made a trip home, spent two days without sleep so I'd look and feel my absolute best for them, rode a bus down to Jacksonville with a lot of local guys, and was shocked at how much Arlo Guthrie called it absolutely perfect in 'Alice's Restaurant.' The guy screaming, 'ALRIGHT. I WANT YOU TO GET OVER HERE AND I WANT YOU TO LINE UP HERE AND . . .' So you walk in a line in your underwear . . .

"I was really lucky because during the student mobilization at Oxford I'd been head of a very small contingent of the Mobilization Committee [National Mobilization Committee to End the War in Vietnam]. My name had got on a list somewhere as a Mobe organizer, and that was around the time Mobe had said, 'Let's organize the army. Let's go inside the army to stop the war.' So they were really watching for Mobe people trying to join the army and my name was already on the list. I said, 'Oh, I was an antiwar organizer. I was a member of Students for a Democratic Society,' and the next thing you know I was walking around with a hot pink card that said 'Commie. Political organizer.'

Saigon during the Tet Offensive.

"That was about it. And then I was put in a trailer for the hearing test and they clapped on earphones and said, 'Punch the button when you hear the tone.' And I'm sitting there waiting and waiting and the next thing I know this big sergeant came back and said, 'You are totally deaf to the tones between so-and-so MHz and so-and-so MHz.' So then I got a yellow card that said 'Infirm.' And so I was put in the group where the sergeant comes in and literally in your face spitting says, 'YOU WILL NOT HAVE THE RIGHT TO DIE FOR YOUR COUNTRY.' And I'm going, 'Hurray. Can you put that in writing?'" —Patrick Edmondson, oral history interview

"I was really naïve going over there; I was thinking I was doing what my country wanted me to do. I was not ashamed of what I was doing, I was looking forward to what I was doing. I was entrusted with a half-million dollar aircraft and had a lot of training under my belt; I had two hundred hours of flight school and I thought I was hotter than hot. It was my job, and I was going to go do it."
—CHARLES CARLSON, ORAL HISTORY INTERVIEW

"Getting off the bird, I think it must have been maybe 8:30 or 9:00 [in the morning], and it must have already been about 90 degrees, 97 degrees . . . So you started sweating immediately. It was like going to your mama's kitchen on Christmas or Thanksgiving Day when she had been cooking turkeys and hams all day, you know, like sweat pouring off you . . . but this ain't your mama's kitchen, man, this is Nam: Welcome to it."
—WILL SMITH, ORAL HISTORY INTERVIEW

"I told my dad, 'You know, Dad, I hope we don't kill all these guys, man, because I want to go.' I wanted to go to war; I was a hawk, man, I wanted to go now . . . So I went to Nam in October and got in my first firefight in November. And what surprised the hell out of me was, these guys fired back. I always thought this was going to be a one-way street, man, that we're just going to be shooting at them. I didn't realize: they're going to be shooting back at us too." —GILBERT DE LA O, ORAL HISTORY INTERVIEW

President Lyndon B. Johnson listens to a tape sent by Captain Charles Robb (his son-in-law) from Vietnam. Both of Johnson's sons-in-law were deployed to avoid perceptions of nepotism.

The 101st Airborne outside Camp Eagle in northern South Vietnam.

"Regardless of your politics, regardless of what you think about the virtue of your service or the difficulties you may have with what you did . . . for all of us who were actually in combat, the sound of [a helicopter's rotor blades] brings you back." —TIM O'BRIEN

"THERE WERE TWO SIDES to [helicopters]—one side was going in to a combat assault where there is nowhere to duck and hide. I remember my company commander, the very first combat assault I was on, he was sitting on the lip of the Huey and I was behind him, kind of in the middle of the helicopter. And he said, 'Grab the straps of my rucksack and hold on.' I said, 'Why?' He said, 'If I'm shot, I don't want to fall out.' I'm thinking, 'If you're shot?!' . . . But there's this exposed thing. The helicopter can't stop the kind of rounds coming at us that close. There's no armor, and no holes to jump in, or nothing to hide behind. There's an exposed feeling that I associate with helicopters when you troop up to get on them, and you know you're going to some bad place, because that's where they wanted to send you, because they didn't send you to happy places. And I couldn't wait to get on the ground so you could duck. On the other hand, a helicopter was a savior at times. The sound of those rotor blades coming in to pull you out of some godawful paddy or out of the mountains somewhere . . . And one minute you're in the war, and then you're out of it and you're up three thousand feet, or however high they go, and you're heading back to some place where at least you aren't getting shot at . . . A few seconds after taking off, you're safe." —Tim O'Brien, oral history interview

"Once you've been through it you're old . . . And I was an old 22-year-old when I returned from there. We expect to confront death when we're 69 or 70 or 80; you don't expect to confront it when you're 21. And you also don't expect to confront it day after day, after day, after day, after day, after day, after day, after day." —TIM O'BRIEN, ORAL HISTORY INTERVIEW

"I felt more confident with the guys, the cats I had been over there with, man . . . All of us got along, man, because nobody wanted to be the last person that died in Vietnam. And that's what we fought for, man, we fought for each other's freedom. We fought for their freedom for one thing, but we fought for ours, just us to be alive and everything; that's what we fought for: for each other."
—WILL SMITH, ORAL HISTORY INTERVIEW

ABOVE: Lance Corporal Ernest Delgado of Los Angeles checks off the months on his tour of duty in Vietnam. LEFT: The 101st Airborne outside Camp Eagle in northern South Vietnam.

"You were very lucky if you were over there and you went in with ten or fifteen people and came out of there with four or five people . . . During a mild week in Vietnam they were losing like 280 people a week. During the whole Tet Offensive in '68, they lost over two or three thousand guys, you know, like within the first two or three months over there . . . I think that we were out there aggressively doing what we were supposed to do, and regardless of what anybody says, we did our best. We thought what we were doing was right, you know." —WILL SMITH

A paraphrase of a popular Marine song, this slogan became widely used by Vietnam veterans in reference to their service.

Interlude
THE MOVING IMAGE

FILM

There have been great single years in Hollywood history—1939, for example, is legendary—and there have been many books about the Oscars, but the Oscar ceremonies of 1968, honoring the prestige pictures of 1967, seemed to sum up the tensions of the year in new ways. Scheduled for April 6, the event was postponed to April 10 that year out of respect for the memory of Martin Luther King, assassinated on April 4 and buried on the ninth. Mark Harris, author of *Pictures at a Revolution,* a book about the five films up for Best Picture that year, writes, "*Bonnie and Clyde* and *The Graduate* were game changers, movies that originated far from Hollywood and had grown into critics' darlings and major popular phenomena; *In the Heat of the Night,* a drama about race, and *Guess Who's Coming to Dinner,* a comedy about race, were middle-of-the-road hits that had, with varying degrees of success, extended a long tradition by addressing a significant social issue within the context of their chosen genres; and *Dr. Dolittle* was a universally dismissed children's musical that most observers felt had bought its way to the final five."

These movies were also among the last made according to the old Motion Picture Production Code, which had ruled Hollywood since the 1930s. By 1968, the Motion Picture Association of America was recommending some films "for mature audiences" and would take this a step further in November by introducing a tiered rating system with levels from G to X. For some, the abandonment of the already-obsolete code might have been further evidence of America's loosening morals. What it cemented was the confusion Harris points to in his summation of the 1967 Oscar nominees:

"What was the American film supposed to be? The men running the movie business used to have the answer; now, it had slipped just beyond their reach, and they couldn't understand how they had lost sight of it . . . The old and the new existed in uneasy proximity, eyeing each other across a red-carpeted aisle that was becoming easy to mistake for a battle line. A fight that began as a contest for a few small patches of Hollywood turf ended as the first shot in a revolution."

The revolution Harris describes continued throughout the next decade of American film, one of Hollywood's most creative and artist focused. Hollywood, like other realms of the popular culture, learned how to take "revolution"—that is, the counterculture—all the way to the bank.

Easy Rider is Exhibit A of this phenomenon. Cowritten by Terry Southern (who had worked with Stanley Kubrick on *Dr. Strangelove*) with the film's stars Dennis Hopper and Peter Fonda, this iconic counterculture "road" movie was in the can by the middle of 1968 but not released until mid-1969 due to a protracted, contentious editing process. *Easy Rider,* like *Bonnie and Clyde,* emitted an aura of violence and coolness as its characters traveled through forgotten parts of the United States. Like *The Graduate,* it featured a groovy soundtrack; *Easy Rider*'s music budget exceeded all other line items. All three films focused on characters on a search for meaning, questioning mainstream values, and suggesting—or violently demonstrating—that such a quest would end badly.

Dennis Hopper, Peter Fonda, and Karen Black filming *Easy Rider* in a Louisiana cemetery. The movie was shot in multiple locations across America over the first half of 1968.

By funding projects like *Easy Rider* for the "youth market," film studios like Columbia Pictures expanded the definition of the mass audience. Still, the mainstream tilted to big-budget musicals like *Oliver!* (1968's Best Picture winner, awarded in 1969) and *Funny Girl,* a big-screen transfer of another huge Broadway hit, the biggest box office success of 1968, eclipsing even the revolutionary *2001: A Space Odyssey.*

1968: Violence As a Way of Life

Other popular films of 1968 seemed to express (as did *2001,* in a more cosmic way) a growing sense of dread and fear of things to come. *Planet of the Apes* suggested that humans would obliterate the known world through nuclear war, leading to the rise of a simian civilization. *Rosemary's Baby* attempted to literalize the horror of the generation gap, as Mia Farrow's character found herself pregnant with the spawn of Satan. George Romero's ultra-low-budget "hippie horror film" *Night of the Living Dead,* released in October, had no time for philosophical dread; it was too full of gruesome violence, a textbook example of the summer movie: cheap and scary, good for the drive-in.

Thrills were also provided that year by Steve McQueen in *Bullitt,* which transformed San Francisco into the backdrop for the most famous car chase in film history: police detective Frank Bullitt (McQueen) in a green fastback Mustang pursuing bad guys in a Dodge Charger. Anyone who saw this movie

Mia Farrow in a still from the 1968 film *Rosemary's Baby,* directed by Roman Polanski. It seemed to capture some of the creeping dread of the year.

when it first came out remembers being blown away by the stomach-churning drops and turns of the chase, which goes on for nearly ten minutes. There is not a word of dialogue, and the jazz score is only there at the beginning—otherwise, it's all screeching tires and revving motors.

There is a lot of violence in *Bullitt,* and it's all intensely *public.* There's always a crowd witnessing the violence or the victims, and the director pans across the craning necks, the milling around, the murmuring. Late in the movie, after Bullitt's girlfriend (Jacqueline Bisset) sees him dealing with a gruesome murder scene, she confronts him with some harsh words, and suddenly he starts to seem less like the maverick antihero and something closer to the Everyman of 1968:

> "With you, living with violence is a way of life, living with violence and death. How can you be part of it, without becoming more and more callous? What will happen to us in time?" Bullitt's answer: "Time starts now."

The Look of 1968

Aside from its San Francisco setting and obsession with violence, *Bullitt* is a quintessentially 1968 film in other ways. One of the pleasures of movies set in the here-and-now of 1968 is being able to revisit that world, so different from our own. When a gangster needs to make a call, he asks the cabbie to pull over at a pay phone. Everyone in the boarding line at a crowded airport is dressed up: men in suits and ties, women in dresses, hats, and stockings. "High-tech" police equipment—shown in close detail—is a copy-transmitting machine that's hooked up to a phone receiver. There's still an Embarcadero Freeway in San Francisco—it was torn down in 1991—and there are still airlines named Pan Am and TWA. Bullitt heats up his instant coffee with an immersion heating coil. ER nurses wear crisp little hats.

While *Bullitt* is still essentially a police procedural, something about its affect and daring makes it feel different, edgy, smart. And Frank Bullitt has that cool disregard for the rules that came to be a standard trope of movie cops. As he says to the unctuous, corrupt politician played by Robert Vaughan, in what became the movie's most-quoted lines, "You believe what you want. You work your side of the street, and I'll work mine." The movie ends abruptly, wordlessly, ambiguously.

Another take on the San Francisco scene was Richard Lester's *Petulia,* invariably included in any list of the most distinctive and "with-it" movies of the moment, along with *Bonnie and Clyde, Rosemary's Baby,* and *The Graduate.* And to dispel any doubts about *Petulia*'s countercultural bona fides, Lester threw in micro-performances by Janis Joplin with Big Brother and the Holding Company and the Grateful Dead and even some groovy colored-oil-and-light show effects. Petulia, played by ravishingly beautiful twenty-six-year-old Julie Christie, is hardly a flower-waving hippie: she's an exceptionally rich San Francisco socialite. There's a bright, jangly texture to *Petulia* and a wonderful use of colorful locations in the San Francisco Bay Area (the requisite cable cars, swanky apartments, Alcatraz, and glamorous parties), but overall, it probably seemed dated even then.
—B.H/E.A.

1968: WHEN MOVIES MATTERED

In 1968 I considered myself an aficionado of movies—and that particular foreign word was one I no doubt tossed around. That was the year, in fact, I declared to my dorm mates at college that "movie critic" was my life's ambition. (I got shot down pretty fast, but that's another story.) By the mid-1960s, I had become one of those millions of Young People who were discovering the illicit pleasures of watching foreign films—*Jules and Jim, Blow-Up, Darling, 8-½*, a slew of depressing Bergman movies—as well as the new, cutting-edge American movies that were also learning from foreign film. We were beginning to understand movies as art forms, as vehicles of personal and cultural expression that really mattered—or, to put it another way, as a means of defining ourselves as outside of the mainstream, as we were also doing with language, dress, and music. As film professor Anthony Schillaci wrote in *Saturday Review,*

> "The better we understand how young people view film, the more we have to revise our notion of what film is. Whether the favored director is 'young' like Richard Lester, Roman Polanski, and Arthur Penn, or 'old' like Kubrick, Fellini, and Bunuel, he must be a practicing cinema anarchist to catch the eye of the young. If we're looking for a young audience . . . we will find they are on a trip, whether in a Yellow Submarine or on a Space Odyssey . . . careening down a dirt road with Bonnie and Clyde or sitting next to The Graduate

as he races across the Bay Bridge. Hyped up on large doses of *Rowan and Martin's Laugh-In,* and *Mission: Impossible,* they are ready for anything that an evolving film idiom can throw on the screen. And what moves them must have the pace, novelty, style, and spontaneity of a television commercial."

Subscribing to *Saturday Review* in 1968 was like a badge of middlebrow sophistication. Reading it made me (a teenager in Texas) feel in touch, East Coast, informed—*cultured,* if only vicariously. A year-end issue in 1968 featured Schillaci's thoughts alongside an op-arty cover hinting at who was "now" in the movies: French director Jean-Luc Godard, American auteur Stanley Kubrick, and serious film stars like Dustin Hoffman (fresh off *The Graduate* and on his way to *Midnight Cowboy* in 1969), Faye Dunaway, Warren Beatty, Mia Farrow, Rod Steiger, among others. To Hollis Alpert, also writing in this issue of the *Saturday Review,* stars were becoming incidental: the Hollywood star system was "crumbling, if not already defunct." Alpert predicted that "the film itself becomes a star, becomes the attracting force for the public." Today's multiplex line-up of superhero spectacles and teen gross-out flicks might attest to the truth of that prediction, though not in the way Alpert had hoped. Indeed, today's movies make a recovering teenage middlebrow like me a little nostalgic for the excitement and sheer hopefulness of the movies of my youth. —B.H.

TELEVISION

". . . to boldly go where no man has gone before."
—*STAR TREK* TITLE SEQUENCE

Despite the claims of television optimists about the potential of the technology to educate, connect, and inform, many people had no interest in being "uplifted" through what had become—in its roughly twenty-year existence—a technology firmly devoted to commercialism and entertainment. Television in 1968 was filled with vapid, escapist entertainments that now take on a queasy unreality when considered in both hindsight and context. Most programming provided no indication that there was anything worrisome or controversial going in either the United States or the world.

The counterculture, racial strife, and the Vietnam War all commanded a good deal of media attention that year. But just as at every other tempestuous period of twentieth-century American history (or, for that matter, twenty-first-century American history), there was a vast cultural mainstream that managed to look away from these uncomfortable realities. Many corny and conventional programs—*My Three Sons, Bonanza, The Lawrence Welk Show, Bewitched, Captain Kangaroo,* and *The Flying Nun*—finished the year stronger than ever. Famously risk averse, networks would not attempt to appeal to younger audiences with "relevant" programming until independent producers Norman Lear, Mary

Captain Kirk, Lieutenant Uhura, and Dr. McCoy wore these insignia on *Star Trek*, whose third and final season began in the fall of 1968.

Tyler Moore, and Grant Tinker approached them in the early 1970s.

Perhaps they were scared by their failure to control the Smothers Brothers. In 1968, their comedy-variety hour (1967–69) became increasingly pointed in its satire and clashed with CBS's censors. As in other struggles that year, it seems likely that if the network hadn't clamped down so ruthlessly, enabling Tom and Dick Smothers to paint themselves as freedom fighters, the whole conflict would have received less attention, particularly from young people who started watching the show *because* it was controversial. To many, the difficulties of the Smothers were emblematic of the difficulties of working within the system. They preferred to "tune in" on a different wavelength.

But topical programming was the exception rather than the rule. Consider some of the top-rated programs of the year: *The Beverly Hillbillies, Bonanza, The Dean Martin Show, A Family Affair, Gunsmoke, Mayberry R.F.D., Here's Lucy,* to name a few. *Gomer Pyle,*

Zebra-print jacket worn by Tom Smothers on *The Smothers Brothers Comedy Hour*. Throughout 1968 Tom and Dick Smothers pushed their variety show in increasingly controversial directions to appeal to their youth audience; the show was abruptly cancelled at the end of the 1968–69 season.

U.S.M.C. was an ostensible comedy about the military that somehow managed to avoid the very war that was dividing the country—and got away with it. The top-rated television shows of 1968 spanned a variety of genres: the fading (the western), the ascendant (the topical drama), and the influx (the sitcom). The most popular variety show that year, gentler in its satire than the Smothers Brothers, was *Rowan and Martin's Laugh-In.*

Laugh-In. All by itself, that hyphenated word—a takeoff on "sit-in" or "be-in," both sixties-invented words—conjures a cascade of 1960s images and memories. Even more specifically, this show has for decades been a stand-in for 1968—or perhaps better, "1968": the pervasive mythologizing of the sixties, a required clip in every sixties montage or even lampoons of sixties montages. Conveniently launching at the beginning of the year (January 22) as NBC's midseason replacement for *The Man from U.N.C.L.E.*—the spy-caper series that had run out of steam—*Rowan and Martin's Laugh-In* soon rocketed to the top of the ratings charts and stayed there for the rest of the season and again for the 1968–69 season. Few other statistics illustrate the

The Flying Fickle Finger of Fate was awarded for dubious achievement on *Rowan and Martin's Laugh-In.*

generation gap as well: CBS's *Gunsmoke* (the iconic western series) and *Here's Lucy* (Lucille Ball's final sitcom), which overlapped with *Laugh-In* on Monday nights, were also in the top ten that year.

With its vibrant, pulsating colors, raunchy or topical joke making, and blindingly quick cuts (over three hundred separate segments in each one-hour show), *Laugh-In* certainly looked and sounded revolutionary and transgressive. But down deep (if that's not an oxymoron in this context), it adhered to formulas familiar to anyone who had been watching TV since its Milton Berle beginnings. It was a variety show, with a strong stock company of players (Goldie Hawn and Lily Tomlin being the show's most famous alumnae); a pair of urbane, tuxedoed hosts; musical acts (the psychedelic band Strawberry Alarm Clock appeared in the opening night's lineup); comic sketches that were long on slapstick and pratfalls; and a boatload of guest stars doing embarrassing things. *Laugh-In* was a curious bit of subversive commodification in which you could often sense the palpable strain of an older generation of industry squares trying desperately to get up to speed as quickly as possible.

Another show that made headlines that year was *Julia,* which debuted with the fall season. The first show to star a black woman who wasn't a maid, *Julia* was part of the "supernegro" trend of the late sixties, along with shows like *I Spy* (with Bill Cosby) and *The Mod Squad,* which, in reaction to decades of racist portrayals, starred black characters so perfect

Promotional portrait of American actor Diahann Carroll wearing a nurse's uniform for the television series *Julia,* the first to star a black woman since *Beulah.*

that they became almost boring. *Julia* was also noteworthy for attempts at period realism: Diahann Carroll's Julia was a professional, working woman (a nurse) and a widow whose husband had been shot down in Vietnam. Although the show was a sitcom, Carroll's character dealt with single motherhood and overt discrimination in the workplace. *Julia* got surprisingly good ratings in its first season, but quickly plummeted out of the top twenty-five in its second, and still further in its final season before being cancelled.

1968 was also the year of Elvis's celebrated comeback special on NBC, but at least the King, performing in black leather, had the class to acknowledge the assassination of Martin Luther King. The Archies, the decidedly not-ready-for-Woodstock cartoon group, premiered on CBS's Saturday morning lineup. The Monkees were still hanging around, although inching ever nearer to a Beatle-esque state of dissolution; their popular television show was cancelled in 1968, and they responded with a feature film, *Head,* that seemed like little more than a bit of trippy career sabotage, though it did feature a cameo by Frank Zappa.

But the universe of television in 1968 cannot be summed up entirely by the dramas, comedies, and variety shows that dominated commercial programming. Most important, perhaps, was the attention devoted to news programs. That summer, CBS and NBC offered "gavel-to-gavel" coverage of the two political conventions, and for the first time all three networks broadcast the proceedings in color. Watching the network news had become a nightly ritual for most Americans, and the anchormen (and they were all men) of the shows were household names and revered celebrities. Television's coverage of Vietnam was vital to the rise and fall of public support for the war, which *New Yorker* writer Michael Arlen called "the living-room war":

> "In 1968, the Vietnam War felt ever more like the central fact in American life . . . a changing shape beneath everything else in that period, in a way that no other war we'd experienced had been, and most of us knew about it, felt about it, from television."

In 1968, television was experimenting, too, with new formats for delivering news and public interest programming. The durable *60 Minutes* debuted that year, billed as a "kind of newsmagazine for television." Throughout the summer, each of the three networks also aired special documentaries about black history and racial unrest in America, produced by their news divisions. The existence and humanity of other racial groups, however, continued to be ignored or avoided: this was the era of the Frito Bandito. After a sojourn to Vietnam following the Tet Offensive, CBS anchor Walter Cronkite was given an entire hour of prime time on February 27, 1968, for a "Report from Vietnam," in which he concluded that the war was "mired in stalemate."

Elsewhere in the television landscape there were other changes on the horizon designed, perhaps, to enrich the soil of the "vast wasteland," as television was notoriously called by FCC chairman Newton Minow in

1961. Congress had just created the Corporation for Public Broadcasting in November 1967, and soon shows like *The French Chef* with Julia Child, already available on small "educational TV" channels, would become PBS staples. Perhaps as another effect of the Kerner Commission's recommendation that broadcasting become more integrated, local and public-access television shows like *Soul!*, *Black Journal*, and *Say Brother* ushered an array of black perspectives onto the airwaves; several of them would make the national jump. In Pittsburgh, a little local show called *Mister Rogers' Neighborhood* went national for the first time in February 1968. A month later in New York, some educators and producers formed an organization they called the Children's Television Workshop; their first effort premiered the following year—*Sesame Street.*
—B.H./B.Z./E.A.

RE-CREATING REALITY

Motorola's future television would be the "electronic heart of the home, dispensing a wide range of goods and services." That prediction came from a special television issue of the *Saturday Evening Post* in November. In the same issue, RCA boasted it could build a television with an eight-foot picture, with "the quality of a travel poster and a three-dimensional effect." Other companies promised future televisions that would be color, or battery-operated, or flat-screened. By the end of 1968, only 25 percent of households had color television (that number would double by 1972).

FCC commissioner Nicholas Johnson acknowledged the plethora of innovations but wondered about the content that would illuminate these gigantic glowing screens, suggesting that, "The future of television is no longer a question of what we can invent. It is a question of what we want." In an article called "Tomorrow's Many-Splendored Tune-In," Sandford Brown pointed out that these companies shared one common goal: "the re-creation of reality in the living room," with a picture so clear and information so instantaneous you would never have to leave your house. With riots, assassinations, and war in Vietnam—not to mention the ever-present fear of the mushroom cloud—staying inside may have sounded pretty good to 1968's Americans.
—B.H.

MARCH The Generation Gap

Saturday
MARCH 4

The *New York Times* runs an article about an anonymous Barnard College coed secretly living off campus with her boyfriend. What became known as the Linda LeClair Affair focused national attention on young people, sexuality, and women's liberation.

Sunday
MARCH 5

A walkout by Mexican American students at two Los Angeles high schools sets in motion a massive protest, eventually involving thousands of students demanding more bilingual education and the teaching of Mexican cultural history.

Sunday
MARCH 10

Labor organizer Cesar Chavez ends a 25-day fast protesting violence against striking migrant farm workers.

"A sexual anthropologist of some future century, analyzing . . . the artifacts of the American sexual revolution, may consider the case of Linda LeClair and her boyfriend, Peter Behr, as a moment when the morality of an era changed." —WILLIAM A. MCWHIRTER, *LIFE*, MAY 1968

Saturday
MARCH 16

Senator Robert Kennedy ends months of speculation by announcing his candidacy for president: "These are not ordinary times, and this is not an ordinary election . . . I need your hand and your help."

•

U.S. soldiers massacre more than 500 Vietnamese civilians in the village of My Lai. An elaborate cover-up suppresses the news for more than a year.

Tuesday
MARCH 12

Minnesota senator Eugene McCarthy comes within a few hundred votes of beating President Lyndon Johnson in New Hampshire's Democratic primary. McCarthy's strong showing is powered by an antiwar message and several thousand student volunteers, who cut their hair and become "clean for Gene" to attract more conservative voters.

Sunday MARCH 17

The Yippies—members of the Youth International Party—hold their first press conference in New York. The Yippies go on to stage numerous theatrical, prank-filled demonstrations against the war and the status quo.

Tuesday MARCH 26

Folksinger and antiwar activist Joan Baez marries draft-resistance organizer David Harris in New York.

Thursday MARCH 28

Dr. Martin Luther King Jr. and followers march in Memphis for sanitation workers' rights. The demonstrations turn violent.

Sunday MARCH 31

President Johnson delivers a nationally televised address to explain a de-escalation of the U.S. bombing campaign in Vietnam. He concludes with a shocking announcement: "I shall not seek, and I will not accept, the nomination of my party for another term as your president."

"I entered the university expecting the Ivy Tower on the Hill—a place where committed scholars would search for truth in a world that desperately needed help. Instead, I found a huge corporation that made money from real estate, government research contracts, and student fees; teachers who cared only for advancement in their narrow areas of study; worst of all, an institution hopelessly mired in the society's racism and militarism." —MARK RUDD, STUDENTS FOR A DEMOCRATIC SOCIETY LEADER AT COLUMBIA UNIVERSITY

"The world was so terrible, we almost didn't really know if we were going to grow up, or want to, because what 'adults' seemed like at that point wasn't something to aspire to." —GRACE LECLAIR, ORAL HISTORY INTERVIEW

UNIVERSITIES HAD GROWN RAPIDLY in the postwar years to accommodate increased demand from the GI Bill, and in 1968 they expanded once again to welcome the children of these GIs. Parents who saw higher education as a path to personal and professional advancement pushed their children to excel and fostered the notion that college would be a high point of their lives. Their children grew to be keenly interested in the self-expression and exploration university life offered. They listened to new music, took new drugs, had intimate relationships facilitated by the availability of oral contraceptives—and even those who didn't could have. Thus, "the generation gap"—already a cliché by 1968.

College students, including these undergraduates at St. Cloud State in Minnesota, embraced the counterculture to differing extents, melding styles and activities in a search for self-expression.

"The '50s was a time when structures were really important, partly, I think, as a reaction to the terrible chaos people experienced in World War II . . . My dad was a Marine in the Pacific. People went through things and then they came back and they were like: 'Thank God we can have refrigerators, we can have jobs, we can have cars, we'll have lots of money, we'll work hard, our wives won't have to work—they can be in the kitchen with their apron and we'll get them a dishwasher if we can. And then our children will be happy—we'll just kind of have happy children.' And if your job is to be a happy child, you're not going to be able to do it." —GRACE LECLAIR

IN FEBRUARY 1968 *Life* magazine, surveying Vietnam, the capture of an American gunship by North Koreans, and, particularly, restless American youth who seemed "more deeply alienated from inherited values than any previous generation," declared, "Wherever we look, something's wrong." But where the editors of *Life,* positioning themselves directly in the mainstream, saw alienation, others saw tradition. In *We Are the People Our Parents Warned Us Against: A Close-Up of the Whole Hippie Scene,* journalist Nicholas von Hoffman challenged the widespread acceptance of "rebellion" as an explanation for the behavior of privileged youth:

> "As a universal explanation the rebellion thesis doesn't hold up, although it's a convenient one for those who would like to avoid discussing the issues that the radicals raise. By defining them as 'youth in rebellion' they can be considered a species of psychological problem and dismissed."

Rather, von Hoffman wrote, many of the young radicals were "carrying out precepts they were taught at home." Raised in privilege by leftist parents, many undergraduates were trying to live the values they had learned within their own families.

EVEN AS ENROLLMENTS ROSE and institutions became more bureaucratic and faceless, colleges clung to their traditional *in loco parentis* role, upholding rules that placed the university in the position of regulating student behavior outside the classroom. Many such rules were designed to keep students, particularly female students, on campus and sheltered from the world that surrounded them. Grace LeClair recalls her first night at Barnard College in New York City:

> "They gathered us all in this living room and it was about 4:30 in the afternoon. And they said, 'We've locked the gates because you don't know where it's safe to walk yet. And so today we're going to explain where it's safe for you to walk, and where it isn't.' So I'm in New York for the first time in my life . . . and we were in prison."

While some universities (particularly those that had grown out of community colleges like San Francisco State or the City University of New York) were engaged with

After 1967's Summer of Love, hippie culture rose to prominence across America.

their communities, most were not. Critic R.W. B. Lewis speculated that "perhaps the most eye-opening experience for the McCarthy students was campaigning in their own cities, of which most of them had known next to nothing." The uproar that arose over LeClair living off campus with her boyfriend was symbolic of the gap between town and gown.

"There are times when order must be maintained because order must be maintained." —GRAYSON KIRK, PRESIDENT OF COLUMBIA UNIVERSITY, 1968

"I'm of another race, not black, not white, maybe I'm of a race that's not here yet, a race without a name. In America you can be a hippy, a doctor, a fireman, but you can't be a man, can't be free." —DAVID SIMPSON, HARVARD DROPOUT, QUOTED BY NICHOLAS VON HOFFMAN

"Vote in the streets!"
—STUDENTS FOR A DEMOCRATIC SOCIETY, 1968

THE STREETS WERE THE ONLY PLACE most college students *could* vote in 1968; the federal voting age was not changed to eighteen until 1971. Moreover, some felt that voting in elections was merely another way to be absorbed into the establishment machine. While Students for a Democratic Society (SDS) mostly made its name through the antiwar protests that characterized 1967, in 1968 they and others inspired by their example brought their confrontational style closer to home. In March and April, Columbia University students shut down their university when discussions about Columbia's involvement in war profiteering and the university's imperial relationship to its Harlem neighbors produced no change.

Other marginalized groups made their presence on campus known in new ways during this period as well. In the spring of 1968 the Negro Affairs Committee at Minnesota's Carleton College renamed itself SOUL (Students Organized toward Unity and Liberation). Black students across the country advocated for black studies departments and more minority representation. While universities were still conservative institutions in '68 and their faculties and administrations were largely supportive of the war in Vietnam, they became increasingly open to accommodating marginalized voices. According to Mark Kurlansky, author of *1968: The Year that Rocked the World,* the popular representation of universities as sanctuaries for "leftist thought and activism . . . is a legacy of the late sixties graduates."

Black students at Carleton College, Northfield, Minnesota.

"If there is one central theme to my campaign, it is the president's duty to liberate individuals so they may determine their own lives, to restore that mastery and power over individual life and social enterprise which has been so seriously eroded by the growing impersonality of our society and by the misuse of central power." —EUGENE MCCARTHY, MARCH 25, 1968

MORALITY SUFFUSED Eugene McCarthy's political persona and his campaign rhetoric. McCarthy's principled reputation enabled him to credibly enter the Democratic presidential primary on a single issue—opposition to President Johnson's conduct of the war in Vietnam—without being accused of showboating. Yet aside from this one arena, McCarthy was mostly a passive candidate, fighting an uphill battle through the winter

ABOVE: Flower Power stickers and dove imagery symbolized youth support for Eugene McCarthy and opposition to the war in Vietnam. RIGHT: Eugene McCarthy campaigned in New Haven, Connecticut, on the heels of his victory in the New Hampshire primary April 3.

of 1967—68 with a team of unseasoned volunteers—widely (and derisively) referred to by political insiders as the Children's Crusade. He placed a surprisingly close second to Johnson in the New Hampshire Democratic primary on March 12.

Excitement about McCarthy's candidacy had spread nationwide by that point; according to Democratic insider John Rauh, "No one cared that McCarthy was awful on domestic affairs. He was right on the war, and the war was everything." Whether McCarthy was, in fact, awful on domestic affairs is debatable, but this was certainly where Robert F. Kennedy felt comfortable challenging him when he entered the primary race four days later,

garnering resentment from many McCarthy supporters. After Kennedy entered the race, McCarthy sighed, "It was politics as usual."

McCarthy's central agenda was to bring an antiwar platform to the Democratic convention. The possibility of actually winning the presidency became concrete when Johnson made the shocking announcement that he would not run for reelection, but McCarthy seemed strangely uninterested in it. Vice President Hubert Humphrey entered the race as the candidate of the party line—and party politics—in April: rather than stumping through Wisconsin, Indiana, Oregon, and California, where he would likely face opposition to his role in the administration's

Prominent celebrities and intellectuals were quick to endorse the campaigns of Kennedy and McCarthy. Here, Paul Newman lends his support to McCarthy's antiwar efforts.

Excitement about McCarthy's candidacy waned when Kennedy entered the primary race.

remarking that McCarthy was heartbroken by the tragedy. He made one speech on the growing violence in American life but remained largely silent, withdrawing from his supporters and from his own campaign.

The McCarthy campaign always seems to raise an odd, perhaps unresolvable tension in those trying to describe it—a tension between a career politician invariably referred to as "aloof," if not "arrogant," and his ground team of enthusiastic young people, seeing in him their best hope for change. Some of the Baby Boomers were eligible to vote for the first time in the 1968 election, but with the federal voting age at twenty-one, most of them were still excluded. Some of the enthusiasm for McCarthy or for the more radical anti-politics of the SDS or Yippies can be traced to this disenfranchisement. McCarthy's single-issue campaign shared its antiwar convictions with these more radical groups, but he profoundly opposed their tactics. His campaign was designed as a way to harness their spirit and bring it back under the control of the Democratic Party.

"Nice and clean for Gene" was an effective campaign slogan as his campaign sought to convince older voters that "straights" could be against the war, too. Though ultimately McCarthy's candidacy has as its legacy political disillusionment and the shattering of the New Deal—era Democratic Party coalition between left-wingers, working-class whites, and racial and ethnic minorities, it should be remembered for something ineffably more positive, as well—what Jeremy Larner called "the humanism of political activity." —E.A.

prosecution of the war, Humphrey dedicated himself and his campaign to pursuing delegates through party organizations. While McCarthy won the Oregon primary, handing Kennedy the first defeat in a decade of family politicking, his supporters' excitement was short lived as the campaign shifted to California in June. McCarthy muffed a debate and lost the primary, but overshadowing everything, Robert Kennedy was assassinated. After Kennedy's death McCarthy's campaign seemed to fall apart, with many observers

These earrings and this dress, worn by a McCarthy supporter, illustrate the merging of politics and style, a signature of the 1960s.

FACING PAGE: Young people came from all over the country to support Eugene McCarthy's antiwar candidacy. To give the movement more credibility, many, like this young man, pledged to "get clean for Gene" by cutting their long hair and beards.

"The dedication and seriousness of the students who canvassed for McCarthy was not only legendary but real. They truly were, as Robert Kennedy was later to point out, the 'A' students in their high schools and colleges. Politically they were inclined to some romanticization of the NLF [National Liberation Front], Che Guevara, and Malcolm X. But whether they came with beards to shave or not, these were kids who reacted against the violent anti-Americanism of the New Left, whom they far outnumbered. Though they hated the war and the draft, they still believed that America could be beautiful—if it would live up to its own principles." —MCCARTHY SPEECHWRITER JEREMY LARNER

APRIL "Something Is Happening in Our World"

Monday 1
APRIL

In Vietnam, the U.S. army launches Operation Pegasus to reopen a land route to the besieged Khe Sanh marine base. The attack by North Vietnamese forces had begun in January and finally ended in the spring. By July, American forces had abandoned the base.

Tuesday 2
APRIL

Stanley Kubrick's mind-blowing film *2001: A Space Odyssey* premieres in Washington, DC.

Thursday 4
APRIL

Civil rights leader Dr. Martin Luther King Jr. is assassinated in Memphis, Tennessee. The news sparks massive riots in hundreds of American cities. King's funeral will be held in Atlanta five days later.

Wednesday 10
APRIL

At the annual Oscar ceremony (postponed four days because of the funeral for Dr. King), the racially charged drama *In the Heat of the Night* beats out *The Graduate*, *Bonnie and Clyde*, *Guess Who's Coming to Dinner*, and *Dr. Dolittle* for best picture of 1967.

"They call me Mister Tibbs!"
—SIDNEY POITIER AS DETECTIVE VIRGIL TIBBS, *IN THE HEAT OF THE NIGHT*

Thursday 11
APRIL

U.S. secretary of defense Clark Clifford calls 24,500 military reservists to action for two-year enlistments and announces a new troop ceiling of 549,500 American soldiers in Vietnam.

•

One week after the death of Dr. King, President Johnson signs into law the Civil Rights Act of 1968, which bans housing discrimination.

Sunday
APRIL 14

Mart Crowley's *The Boys in the Band*, a dark comedy about a group of gay men, opens off-Broadway at Theater Four and establishes a new genre.

Tuesday
APRIL 23

To protest Columbia University's affiliation with the Institute for Defense Analysis, students occupy the school's administration building. The action culminates seven days later when police storm the building and violently remove students and their supporters.

Saturday
APRIL 27

Following weeks of speculation, Vice President Hubert H. Humphrey announces his candidacy for the presidency in front of a crowd of 1,700 supporters in Washington, DC.

Monday
APRIL 29

The countercultural musical *Hair* opens on Broadway, sparking controversy over its profanity and nudity, its celebration of illegal drugs, and its open irreverence for the American flag.

"I think we thought that if we try hard, keep ourselves clean, behave, then whites will see what good people we are and they will not discriminate against us. It was a question of lifting yourself up, improving the race, and that will kind of undermine racism. It was assumed that racism was rational and that there was something that we could do to improve ourselves. Dress well, study hard, excel, and eventually things will get better."

—CAROLE MERRITT, FORMER STUDENT NONVIOLENT COORDINATING COMMITTEE ACTIVIST, ORAL HISTORY INTERVIEW

THE RELEASE OF THE *Report of the National Advisory Commission on Civil Disorders,* popularly known as the Kerner Commission Report, presented Americans with some uncomfortable truths about the riots that had rocked hundreds of cities in the summers of 1965, 1966, and 1967. Unlike previous government reports, and contrary to popular attitudes, this report identified structural and institutional racism as the root of the racial unrest. The report offered specific recommendations to both government and media, charging the media with finding "ways of exploring the problems of the Negro and the ghetto . . . honestly, realistically, and imaginatively," and linking federal programs to the goals of civil rights leaders. The report identified a movement "toward two societies, one black, one white" that both characterized and perhaps pushed even further the polarizations of 1968, enabling candidates like Richard Nixon and George Wallace to firmly position themselves on the white side.

In racial justice circles, the reports verified the continuing presence of racism in American life and the necessity for federal intervention that leaders like Martin Luther King Jr. continued to push for.

"I can imagine that had [Dr. King] lived for maybe two more years, we might have made even greater strides toward the kind of equality and the understanding that the country really needs. I still don't think we have the understanding. And the equality is shaky too." —BRENDA BANKS, ARCHIVIST, ORAL HISTORY INTERVIEW

ABOVE: Nonviolent protesters often met violent resistance from law enforcement and fellow citizens; here, high school student Taylor Washington is arrested at Lebs Delicatessen in Atlanta, Georgia—his eighth arrest. FACING PAGE: While hundreds of urban residents acted out their grief violently on the nights following Dr. King's assassination, the uprisings in Chicago (pictured here) and Washington, DC, became the most notorious.

THE KERNER REPORT reminded an America that needed no reminding of the past three summers of violence, and American cities braced for another one. When Dr. King was assassinated on April 4, summer came early. People acted out their grief and anger in an outbreak of violent uprisings that took place in hundreds of cities. King had made nonviolence an American civil virtue, and it was ironic how quickly that virtue went by the wayside with his death and the extent to which blacks turned their anger against their own neighborhoods. Uprisings in Indianapolis and Boston were diminished, if not forestalled entirely, by the words of Robert F. Kennedy and James Brown, but Chicago, Washington, DC, Oakland, and more than forty other places went up in flames. —E.A.

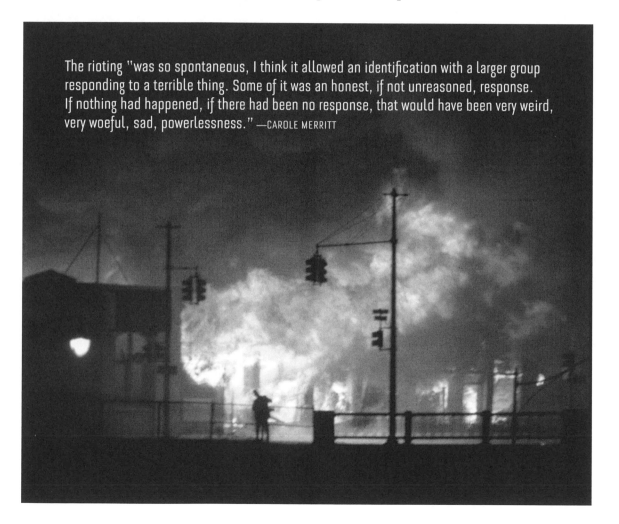

The rioting "was so spontaneous, I think it allowed an identification with a larger group responding to a terrible thing. Some of it was an honest, if not unreasoned, response. If nothing had happened, if there had been no response, that would have been very weird, very woeful, sad, powerlessness." —CAROLE MERRITT

JAMES BROWN: SOUL POWER/BLACK POWER

Black Power made an indelible mark on America in 1968, but for all the high-profile antics and incendiary rhetoric of the Black Panthers, the two men who best represented Black Power on a national scale made their mark in other arenas: Muhammad Ali and James Brown.

By 1968 neither was yet the widespread cultural icon he would later become, but the two men were unquestionably black superstars who had already made an impression on the white mainstream. They were opinionated and outspoken, politically engaged, and smart and colorful enough to attract attention with their public statements.

By 1968 Ali had embraced Islam, changed his name from Cassius Clay, twice vanquished Sonny Liston for the World Boxing Council's heavyweight title, and allegedly thrown his Olympic gold medal into the Ohio River after being refused service at a restaurant. He had also, in 1966, publicly refused to serve in the Vietnam War, explaining with characteristic candor, "I ain't got no quarrel with the Vietcong. No Vietcong ever called me nigger." Ali was stripped of his title belt in 1967 as punishment for his opposition to the war and resistance to the draft.

As for Brown, in 1968 he was at the peak of his powers—he would always be great, but he was never better, never more vital and plugged-in to what was happening in the country. He released eight albums on King Records that year, including the astonishing second installment of *Live at the Apollo* and the remarkably timely single "Say It Loud, I'm Black and I'm Proud," which managed to distill the rhetoric of all the then-divergent voices

James Brown performing.

of the civil rights movement into two minutes and fifty-nine seconds of concise, righteous, and utterly danceable funk.

According to Brown's 1968 autobiography, he had been an early confidante of then vice president Hubert Humphrey and had warned Humphrey for several years about growing unrest in the inner cities; he was seeing it at his concerts and hearing rumors on the grapevine and feared that "there was going to be a bloodbath." He also recounts a 1967 meeting with activist H. Rap Brown backstage at Harlem's Apollo Theater. "I'm not going to tell anyone to pick up a gun," he told Brown, who was then chairman of the Student Nonviolent Coordinating Committee. "Even if we did start a revolution, our people couldn't do nothing but lose. We're outgunned and we're outnumbered."

On April 5, 1968, James Brown had a concert scheduled at the Boston Garden. Martin Luther King Jr. had been assassinated in Memphis the previous day, and Boston was rocked by riots. There were similar violent eruptions in cities all over the country, and President Johnson had declared a state of emergency.

Boston mayor Kevin White contemplated cancelling Brown's performance out of fear of fanning the unrest. There was a risk either way, and White, along with the city council and Brown and his man-

agers, came up with a plan to stage a live broadcast of the concert on WGBH, the local public television station, in the hopes that it would keep people off the streets. The plan worked spectacularly; the crime rate was down in Boston that night even by the standards of any other Friday night.

The concert itself did not go off without tense moments, however, despite Brown's repeated pleas to the audience to remain calm and honor the memory of Dr. King. At some point in Brown's performance audience members began to rush the stage, and Boston police responded with force in an attempt to remove them. According to Brown's autobiography and period accounts from the local papers, Brown stopped his band and asked the police to step back. "I think I can get some respect from my own people," he reportedly said. And then he shook hands with the stage crashers and politely asked them to leave the stage. Which they did.

There were continuing riots all over America that night, but there were no riots in Boston. —B.Z.

. . . .

"Martin Luther King was executed by a firing squad that numbered in the millions. They took part from all over the country, pouring words of hate into the ear of the assassin . . . So we killed him. Just as we killed Abraham Lincoln and John F. Kennedy. No other country kills so many of its best people . . . We have pointed a gun at our own head and we are squeezing the trigger." —MIKE ROYKO, *CHICAGO DAILY NEWS*, APRIL 5, 1968

"Even more harrowing for me was when he was brought back to Atlanta and his body lay in state at the Spelman College Sisters Chapel and thousands of people lined up on campus to view the body. And you would think that you would hear noise: you could hear a pin drop on that campus. I mean, it was absolutely quiet. It was an amazing thing. To this day, I can't understand how so many people could be so quiet. And I think it was out of respect and grief. But it was eerie, it was really eerie. Everything just stopped, and the only thing moving was the line that snaked throughout the whole campus."

—BRENDA BANKS, ORAL HISTORY INTERVIEW

Mourners in Minneapolis honoring King.

AS BEFITTED A MAN known for his oratory, King's own words were played at his funeral, the audio taken from a particularly morbid sermon he had given at Ebenezer Baptist Church two months earlier:

"If any of you are around when I have to meet my day, I don't want a long funeral. And if you get somebody to deliver the eulogy, tell them not to talk too long. And every now and then I wonder what I want them to say. Tell them not to mention that I have a Nobel Peace Prize—that isn't important. Tell them not to mention that I have three or four hundred other awards—that's not important. Tell them not to mention where I went to school. I'd like somebody to mention that day that Martin Luther King Jr. tried to give his life serving others. I'd like for somebody to say that day that Martin Luther King Jr. tried to love somebody.

I want you to say that day that I tried to be right on the war question. I want you to be able to say that day that I did try to feed the hungry. And I want you to be able to say that day that I did try in my life to clothe those who were naked. I want you to say on that day that I did try in my life to visit those who were in prison. I want you to say that I tried to love and serve humanity. Yes, if you want to say that I was a drum major, say that I was a drum major for justice. Say that I was a drum major for peace. I was a drum major for righteousness. And all of the other shallow things will not matter."

Front page of the *Atlanta Inquirer,* Atlanta's largest black newspaper, April 20, 1968.

"The focus on [King] alone is misleading . . . because it misses the point of the civil rights movement. It was a movement. It was about people organizing for change. Leadership was important. But what the history and the curriculum forget is that it would not have happened if there wasn't a community that was transformed to organize in the way that it did. Not the entire community, but enough in the community who were willing to say, 'I am not afraid. We're going to challenge white power, white-sanctioned violence. We're going to stare that in the face without guns.' That's a phenomenal story. That's a phenomenal faith in each other and in God. And it worked. It worked. King you've got to have. He's essential, he's an exceptional person. But what I needed then, and what I think young people need now, is some understanding of what they as communities did, as *communities*." —CAROLE MERRITT, ORAL HISTORY INTERVIEW

. . . .

THE ASSASSINATION OF MARTIN LUTHER KING, AND THE AFTERMATH

By 1968 the country was confronting mounting criticism of the Vietnam War, demonstrations at campuses and in cities all over the country, and the emergence of a Black Power movement that renounced the nonviolence and civil disobedience so long espoused by Martin Luther King Jr. and his Southern Christian Leadership Conference. Meanwhile King himself had turned his attention to the Poor People's Campaign and the issue of poverty in America.

King was only thirty-nine years old, but it was apparent that he was exhausted by his long battles and by the dramatic escalation of overt hostility in both the civil rights movement and the culture at large. Behind him already were some of the greatest triumphs of principled protest, organized dissent, and civil disobedience in the history of the country: the Montgomery bus boycott (1955), the March on Washington and his timeless "I Have a Dream" speech (1963), "Letter from a Birmingham Jail" (1963), the march from Selma to Montgomery (1965), and his condemnation of the Vietnam War at the Riverside Church in New York (1967). In 1964 he had become the youngest ever recipient of the Nobel Peace Prize. That same year President Johnson signed the Civil Rights Act, which was followed in 1965 by the passage of the Voting Rights Act. King had played a major role in the desegregation of schools, the establishment of fair housing laws, and the ban on racial discrimination by federal agencies.

On April 3 of 1968 King was in Memphis. The reason for his visit was modest and somewhat startling given everything else that was going on in the country: He was there to lead a demonstration on behalf of 1,300 striking sanitation workers. His flight into Memphis was delayed by a bomb threat, and when he finally arrived he delivered what was to be his last speech to a small crowd that had gathered despite the inclement weather.

"Well, I don't know what will happen now," King told his audience, in what surely ranks as one of the most chillingly prescient speeches ever delivered. "We've got some difficult days ahead. But it really doesn't matter with me now, because I've been to the mountaintop. And I don't mind. Like anybody, I would like to live a long life—longevity has its place. But I'm not concerned about that now. I just want to do God's will. And He's allowed me to go up to the mountain. And I've looked over, and I've seen the Promised Land. I may not get there with you. But I want you to know tonight, that we, as a people, will get to the Promised Land. And so I'm happy tonight; I'm not worried about anything; I'm not fearing any man. Mine eyes have seen the glory of the coming of the Lord."

The next day he was in room 306 at the Lorraine Motel, a decidedly modest two-story motor court, preparing a sermon entitled, "America May Go to Hell." He shaved and dressed and prepared to have dinner with his traveling party and a local minister. As King stepped out onto the balcony and began to descend the stairs he was struck in the head by a single shot from a .30-06 caliber rifle. Shortly after seven that evening he was pronounced dead at a local hospital. In one of his pockets was a quote from Mahatma Gandhi that King allegedly always carried: "In the midst of death, life persists. In the midst of darkness, life persists."

That night, as word of King's assassination spread across the country, there were riots in forty American cities, with widespread burning and looting. Chicago's pugnacious mayor, Richard Daley, gave his police a shoot-to-kill order. Twelve were killed in Washington, DC.

Two funerals were held in Atlanta on April 9, the first at Ebenezer Baptist Church, where King had followed his father into the pulpit and delivered some of his most stirring rhetoric, and the second at King's alma mater, Morehouse College. The casket was transported from Ebenezer to Morehouse aboard a farm wagon drawn by two mules, and tens of thousands of silent observers lined the funeral route.

It was 1968, and the country seemed to be coming apart, along with everything Martin Luther King Jr. had spent his life fighting for.

In the immediate aftermath of King's death Stokely Carmichael uttered the words that indicated both how much had changed and how much had been forever lost: "Now that they've taken Dr. King off, it's time to end this non-violent bullshit."

Three months later Bobby Kennedy would be gunned down in Los Angeles, and all the hope of 1968 evaporated. —B.Z.

. . . .

"But I know, somehow, that only when it is dark enough, can you see the stars. Something is happening in our world. The masses of people are rising up. And wherever they are assembled today, whether they are in Johannesburg, South Africa; Nairobi, Kenya; Accra, Ghana; New York City; Atlanta, Georgia; Jackson, Mississippi; or Memphis, Tennessee, the cry is always the same: 'We want to be free.'" —MARTIN LUTHER KING JR., APRIL 3, 1968, MEMPHIS

RIGHT, TOP: Placard carried by marchers memorializing King.
RIGHT, BOTTOM: Program from King's funeral.

MAY "I Am Somebody"

Thursday MAY 2

The Boston Celtics beat the Los Angeles Lakers to win their tenth National Basketball Association championship title.

Saturday MAY 4

Dancer's Image, in a thrilling last-minute finish, wins the Kentucky Derby but is disqualified three days later after testing positive for a painkilling drug. The colt is the only Derby winner in history to have its crown taken away. *Sports Illustrated* calls the scandal the "sporting story of the year."

Monday MAY 6

William Styron, a white author, is awarded the Pulitzer Prize in fiction for *The Confessions of Nat Turner*, based on the true story of an 1831 slave revolt in Virginia. Ten black authors write essays criticizing the work, collected in *William Styron's Nat Turner: Ten Black Writers Respond*.

Friday MAY 10

Following a ban on demonstrations and the closure of universities and sections of central Paris, thousands of students hit the streets to protest. Riot police refuse to allow demonstrators to cross the Left Bank, the crowd creates makeshift barricades, and a battle ensues.

•

U.S. and North Vietnamese negotiators meet in Paris for the opening session of talks intended to end the conflict in Vietnam. The talks stall for five months, as neither Hanoi nor Washington is willing to make concessions that would allow full negotiations to begin.

"Be realistic—demand the impossible."
—SITUATIONIST GRAFFITI, PARIS

Saturday MAY 11

Dr. Ralph Abernathy, successor to Dr. Martin Luther King Jr., and the Southern Christian Leadership Conference are granted a permit for an encampment on the Mall in Washington, DC. Eventually more than 6,000 people occupy Resurrection City—a shantytown filled with poor people of all races.

FBI director J. Edgar Hoover sends all field offices an urgent memo authorizing an operation called "Counterintelligence Program—New Left" (or COINTELPRO). It is one of a series of covert projects aimed at infiltrating, discrediting, and disrupting domestic political organizations.

•

In New York City, the Beatles announce the formation of Apple Corps, a multimedia conglomerate. Paul McCartney calls it a "beautiful place to buy beautiful things."

Saturday MAY 25

The Gateway Arch, part of the Jefferson National Expansion Memorial in St. Louis, is dedicated by vice president Hubert Humphrey and interior secretary Stewart Udall.

Friday MAY 17

In Maryland, a group of activists who come to be known as the Catonsville Nine—including Catholic priests Daniel Berrigan, Philip Berrigan, and Thomas Melville—take hundreds of files from a local draft board and set them on fire with gasoline and homemade napalm in protest of the Vietnam War.

"I saw that if you are poor in Mississippi and you are poor in North Dakota, it's all the same thing. You're fighting the same battle." —TILLY WALKER, ORAL HISTORY INTERVIEW, 1968

"We've got to massively confront the power structure . . . This is a move to dramatize the situation, channelize the very legitimate and understandable rage of the ghetto and we know we can't do it with something weak. It has to be something strong, dramatic, and attention-getting." —MARTIN LUTHER KING JR., IN A 1967 PRESS CONFERENCE ANNOUNCING PLANS FOR THE POOR PEOPLE'S CAMPAIGN

Aerial view of the shantytown known as Resurrection City, located parallel to the National Mall in Washington, DC (photo shows Lincoln Memorial and Arlington Bridge at top right).

RESURRECTION CITY was planned to be a protest that would demand the nation's attention: thousands of poor Americans camping on the National Mall, putting the experiences of rural and urban poor people at the center of the national consciousness. The plywood city, built in the shadow of the Washington Monument, was meant to shock Americans into taking issues of poverty—across racial lines—seriously. Organized by Reverend Martin Luther King Jr. and the Southern Christian Leadership Conference, the goal of the project was to wrest a "Bill of Economic Rights" from Congress through a militant camp-in where

people from all of the nation's poor communities would literally bring poverty to the front doorstep of the nation's lawmakers. The Poor People's Campaign was conceived inclusively; Dr. Bernard Lafayette recalled planning with King, asking him,

> "'Are you talking about getting Hispanics involved?' He said, 'Yes!' 'What about Native Americans?' 'Yes!' So I was getting to the final question, and that was the poor whites from Appalachia . . . He said, 'Are they poor?' I said, 'Yes.' He said if they were poor then this was their campaign."

This sign was used at Resurrection City, possibly in one of the residents' daily protest marches.

After King's assassination, Reverend Ralph David Abernathy assumed leadership of the Southern Christian Leadership Conference and its Poor People's Campaign.

"We want food for the hungry. We want jobs for the jobless. We want justice for the oppressed. We want housing for the ill-housed. And we want doctors and medicine for those who are ill . . . I could put it another way if you choose. We believe in the dignity of man. And we believe that no man can have true dignity unless all men have it."

—RALPH ABERNATHY

WHEN KING WAS SHOT in April, most of the project's momentum was lost. As riots exploded across America, many of the campaign's backers believed that the potential for violence in Resurrection City was too great and wanted to cancel the project. But King's successor, Reverend Ralph Abernathy and the SCLC reached out to other racial and ethnic movements to build coalitions transcending race for the sake of economic justice.

The tents of Resurrection City saw many prominent visitors, including James Brown.

"'It was the first time that a lot of us had any contact with Puerto Ricans, with Appalachian whites. When you never have been out of the state . . . never like even over one hundred miles from where you were born, to come in contact with all these people and these different cultures and these different subcultures,' it was an education far beyond any classroom." —GORDON MANTLER, QUOTING CHICANO ACTIVIST RALPH RAMÍREZ

CARAVANS FROM ACROSS the nation began arriving in mid-May, with 6,312 people eventually enrolling as official residents of the plywood shantytown. Leaders Jesse Jackson and Hosea Williams led groups of hundreds of people to protest at different governmental agencies each day. But the weather quickly turned against them, bringing an onslaught of rain that doused the National Mall. The rain, characterized as biblical by many participants, created such poor conditions that Resurrection City soon became, ironically, indistinguishable from a slum. Permanent toilets were never completed, and showers were in construction until the last week of the campaign. Doctors worked overtime to prevent the outbreak of disease. Cars were abandoned, and calf-deep pools of mud developed in the alleyways between plywood homes.

On June 19 Reverend Abernathy declared a "Solidarity Day" march, which drew the attention of the nation as an estimated 50,000 people marched in the footsteps of Dr. King's famous 1963 March on Washington. Although police presence was high, the march was successful at maintaining its nonviolent goals.

Reverend Jesse Jackson, one of the "mayors" of Resurrection City, on the grounds.

Shortly after Solidarity Day the permit for Resurrection City was revoked, and on June 23 the police cleared the city. Within a few days it had been completely dismantled and stood empty. Abernathy and those who refused to leave were arrested. The Poor People's Campaign was lauded as an ambitious project but summed up in one reflective *New York Times* headline: "Poor People's Drive Makes Gains, but Fails to Reach Goals." The campaign did not achieve an Economic Bill of Rights, but Resurrection City did create connections between young activists, many of whom remained dedicated to the cause of eliminating poverty for many years to come. —M.N.

Conditions in Resurrection City were rudimentary at best, with one central pump providing water.

PARIS, MAY 1968

Alongside the protests at Columbia University in April, the events that have become embedded in the French consciousness as Mai '68 are a prime example of a trend Mark Kurlansky has identified as characteristic of the year. In many ways, French society was primed for this uprising just as American society had been: a student body radicalized by colonial war (in this case, Algeria), a skyrocketing number of students, and overcrowded universities that clung to hierarchical traditions. As in the United States and other countries, student leaders and icons would emerge not because of careful planning or democratic election but almost by chance. When Daniel Cohn-Bendit (soon to be known internationally as "Dany le Rouge" for the correspondence between his hair and his politics) spoke out against the cloistering of female students at the suburban University of Nanterre, the French university system responded by calling him to Paris for a disciplinary hearing. This miscalculation enabled him to take his message of student freedom and liberation to a much wider audience, shutting down not only Nanterre but also the Sorbonne, and from there, the streets of Paris.

While the students' lack of organization and direction made forging alliances unlikely—and, in fact, was off-putting to French union leaders and

"It is remarkable how many of the movements of 1968 took on importance only because governments or university administrations adopted repressive measures to stop them. Had they instead ignored them . . . many would have been forgotten today."
—MARK KURLANSKY, *1968: THE YEAR THAT ROCKED THE WORLD*

Communist Party officials—their willingness to strike, to battle police, and to use the media to make their case opened a space for dialogue and also encouraged political protest by other groups. The workers of France (whatever their qualms about the students' commitment to economic justice) joined them in a wildcat general strike that shut down Paris and the rest of the country until President Charles De Gaulle could call for new elections that enabled him, though weakened, to stay in power.

What was surprising about the violence in France was how few people died. While police brutality was rampant here as elsewhere, it managed to remain well within the limits that would have prompted full-scale revolution. Mai '68 is better remembered for its situationist slogans and marathon conversations than for any lasting political or social changes, which may have ultimately been the students' goal anyway. —E.A.

The banners and graffiti of Mai '68 and Resurrection City became icons in their own right.

THE WALLS HAVE EARS, AND VOICES

Absent computers, Photoshop, Kinko's, digital cameras, or cell phones, 1968 nonetheless produced countless examples of agitprop art and expression that were reproduced on mimeograph machines, silk screens, T-shirts, and other countercultural commodities. It was a year of countless acronyms, slogans, and inspired graffiti flourishes that appeared—with remarkably little time lag—on walls all over the world. The year arguably represented the last heyday of widely disseminated propaganda in the form of street art, pamphlets, and placards.

Situationist and enragé philosophers, protesters, and artists in France managed to combine a European sensibility and aphoristic rigor with the blunt and often deliberately offensive outrage of their American counterparts, and many of their slogans and graffiti tags were appropriated or adapted by the more cerebral cadre of dissenters on the other side of the Atlantic. The terse, exclamatory art of the 1968 revolutionaries pointed the way to the black humor that exploded in literature and film, the clipped, angry anthems of punk rock, and even the mantras of the self-help movement.

Looking at one large collection of the graffiti that appeared in Paris and Prague in 1968, it's astonishing how fresh, funny, and contemporary (not to mention prescient) so much of it still feels:

Freedom is the crime that contains all crimes.

The spectacle is everywhere!

Only the truth is revolutionary.

Down with the spectacle-commodity society!

You can no longer sleep quietly once you've opened your eyes.

The future will only contain what we put into it now.

Long live communication; down with telecommunication.

Talk to your neighbors.

Look in front of you.

Yell.

Write everywhere.

I have something to say, but I don't know what.

Create.

I participate. You participate. We participate. They profit.

Constraints imposed on pleasure incite the pleasure of living without constraints.

Going through the motions kills the emotions.

Your ears have walls.

When examined, answer with questions.

Professors, you make us grow old.

Form dream committees.

Life is elsewhere.

Action must not be a reaction, but a creation.

Be realistic, demand the impossible.

—B.Z.

JUNE Violence Shock

Sunday 3
JUNE

Valerie Solanas, founder of the Society for Cutting Up Men (SCUM), shoots famed pop artist Andy Warhol in his New York film studio. Warhol survives, and Solanas, after pleading guilty, is sentenced to three years in a psychiatric facility.

"Life in this society being, at best, an utter bore and no aspect of society being at all relevant to women, there remains to civic-minded, responsible, thrill-seeking females only to overthrow the government, eliminate the money system, institute complete automation, and destroy the male sex."

—VALERIE SOLANAS,
"THE SCUM MANIFESTO"

Wednesday 5
JUNE

Senator Robert F. Kennedy is shot and mortally wounded in Los Angeles just after claiming victory in California's Democratic presidential primary. Gunman Sirhan Bishara Sirhan, a Palestinian American, is immediately arrested. Kennedy dies in a hospital the next day.

Friday 7
JUNE

In Spain, members of ETA, a Basque separatist group, shoot and kill a military policeman at a checkpoint, marking ETA's first killing in its fight for independence.

Saturday 8
JUNE

A little more than two months after the murder of Dr. Martin Luther King Jr., suspected assassin and white supremacist James Earl Ray is captured at London's Heathrow airport. Ray is extradited and charged. After eventually pleading guilty, he is sentenced to 99 years in prison.

Wednesday 12
JUNE

Rosemary's Baby, a horror film written and directed by Roman Polanski, is released. The film, Polanski's first English-language movie, receives mostly favorable reviews and earns numerous nominations and awards.

Thursday **13**
JUNE

Earl Warren, Chief Justice of the United States since 1954, submits his resignation to President Johnson but stays on the Supreme Court until January 1969. The Warren Court was responsible for landmark decisions in racial segregation, the right to privacy, and due process under the law.

Friday **14**
JUNE

Famed pediatrician and author Dr. Benjamin Spock and three other activists, including Yale university chaplain William Sloane Coffin Jr., are convicted in a federal district court in Boston of conspiring to aid, abet, and counsel draft registrants to "violate the Selective Service Act," that is, to resist conscription into the military.

Wednesday **19**
JUNE

On Solidarity Day nearly 50,000 people march through Washington, DC, in support of the Poor People's Campaign to end poverty. Five days later bulldozers move in and demolish the huge encampment known as Resurrection City.

Friday **28**
JUNE

Aretha Franklin—1968's best-selling female recording artist—hits the cover of *Time*.

•

In Berkeley, California, 2,000 people attend a rally in support of radical students in France. Police escalate crowd-control tactics to unprecedented levels and a street war breaks out, replete with flaming barricades, citywide curfews, and hundreds of arrests.

Robert F. Kennedy reaching out to supporters shortly after announcing his candidacy.

"These are not ordinary times and this is not an ordinary election." —ROBERT F. KENNEDY CAMPAIGN BROCHURE

IT'S EASY TO FORGET how very brief Robert Kennedy's 1968 presidential campaign was. He had only declared his intention to seek the nomination on March 16—after Eugene McCarthy's surprising show of strength in the New Hampshire primary on March 12 but before the famous announcement by President Johnson that he would not be seeking a second term, opening up space for Vice President (and eventual nominee) Hubert H. Humphrey, who announced at the end of April.

Kennedy's announcement speech sounded many of the themes that would characterize his campaign:

> "I run because I am convinced that this country is on a perilous course and because I have such strong feelings about what must be done, and I feel that I'm obliged to do all that I can . . . I run to seek new policies— policies to end the bloodshed in Vietnam and in our cities, policies to close the gaps that now exist between black and white, between rich and poor, between young and old, in this country and around the rest of the world. I run because it is now unmistakably clear that we can change these disastrous, divisive policies only by changing the men who are now making them."

Even absent the King assassination and the destructive riots that followed in the first weekend in April, the political atmosphere of 1968 could feel more than a little gloomy: a wounded Johnson brooding in the White House; a McCarthy campaign failing to capitalize on its initial enthusiasm; divisive and mean-spirited words from the George Wallace camp; and over in the Republican corner, the glowering, shifty-looking front-runner, Richard Nixon.

Kennedy—by far the youngest of any of the hopefuls—brought in fresh waves of optimism to huge swaths of the electorate, along with the trademark magic and show-biz glamour of the Kennedy family name. Celebrity endorsements of candidates were getting

Kennedy campaigning in Los Angeles, where he awaited the results of the California primary.

"THE HAPPY WARRIOR"

1968 was—or should have been—Hubert Humphrey's year, but for him the year's narrative reads more like classical tragedy. In March Lyndon Johnson, under brutal pressure from his critics for a failing war in Vietnam, decided not to run for a second term as president. A full month later, Humphrey—facing stiff opposition from two antiwar Democratic senators, Eugene McCarthy and Robert Kennedy—threw his hat into the ring, announcing that his would be a "politics of joy." (Even some of his supporters, however, were embarrassed by this display of ebullience coming just three weeks after the murder of Dr. King.)

McCarthy's campaign stumbled, Kennedy was killed in early June, and Humphrey emerged as the front-runner for the nomination, though still fighting to become his own man, independent of the twinned curse of Johnson and Vietnam. The nominating convention in Chicago in late August became a near disaster both inside and outside the convention hall, with pitched battles between out-of-control Chicago police and violent, angry, antiwar hippies and Yippies spoiling for a fight. Humphrey emerged a winner but was severely bruised by the riots and Democratic disarray.

His presidential campaign—just a little more than two months long—was rocky and further complicated by the strong presence of arch-segregationist and former Alabama governor George Wallace,

running as a third-party candidate. Humphrey lagged behind for a while, then pulled close in the waning days of October, only to lose to Nixon on November 5. The popular vote tally was extremely close—the two were separated by less than 1 percent—but Nixon prevailed decisively in the electoral college. It was a bitter disappointment for Humphrey—the Happy Warrior—who had twice before sought the Democratic nomination and had served as such a loyal soldier under the difficult, domineering Lyndon Johnson. After a few years out of the political spotlight, Humphrey again ran for the Senate, where he had served from 1949 to 1964, and was elected in 1970 and again in 1976.

"The future has several names. For the weak, it is the impossible. For the faint-hearted, it is the unknown. For the thoughtful and the valiant, it is the ideal. The challenge is urgent, the task is large, the time is now. Here we are, the way politics ought to be in America: the politics of happiness, the politics of purpose, the politics of joy. And that's the way it's going to be, too, from here on out!" —HUBERT H. HUMPHREY, QUOTING VICTOR HUGO AND ANNOUNCING HIS CANDIDACY FOR PRESIDENT, APRIL 27, 1968

The centennial of Hubert H. Humphrey's birth was celebrated in 2011. He shares a birth year with another towering figure in American political history, Ronald Reagan. At one time early in their public lives the two men actually occupied roughly the same side of the political spectrum—the liberal Democratic side. Reagan swung far to the right by the 1950s, becoming the great standard-bearer of American conservatism. Humphrey, however, remained devoted to liberal political ideals—especially civil rights, education, and jobs programs—until his dying day, which sadly came too soon, in January 1978, when he was only sixty-six. —B.H.

more ink than ever in 1968—movie stars Paul Newman and Tony Randall campaigned for McCarthy in New Hampshire, and Nixon would gain the public support of movie star John Wayne, basketball giant Wilt Chamberlain, and football hero Bart Starr—but no one attracted more sheer star wattage than Kennedy. His campaign could (and did) boast a staggering lineup of famous-name supporters, everyone from box-office leaders Warren Beatty and Sidney Poitier to Andy Warhol, Hank Aaron, Vince Lombardi, Truman Capote, and Diana Ross and the Supremes.

Upon entering the race in mid-March, Kennedy had to overcome a considerable amount of resentment by McCarthy supporters, who saw Kennedy's bid as pure opportunism. When Johnson bowed out of the race, the field was for weeks divided between Kennedy and McCarthy, both running on an antiwar platform. The resentful McCarthy proved to be an indifferent campaigner, and Kennedy—firing much more excitement among Democratic voters—surged ahead in the polls.

McCarthy and Kennedy went head-to-head in several primary races (Vice President Humphrey, entering the race at the end of April, did not contest any primaries), but the big win—California—went to Kennedy on June 4. Just after midnight, following a brief speech claiming victory at the Ambassador Hotel in Los Angeles, Kennedy was mortally wounded in a shooting in the hotel's kitchen. Nearly twenty-six hours later, on June 6, Kennedy was declared dead.

Ambassador Hotel busboy Juan Romero attempts to comfort a dying Kennedy in the hotel's kitchen.

The gunman was a twenty-four-year-old Palestinian Christian, Sirhan Bishara Sirhan, a U.S. resident since he was twelve, who had become obsessed with Kennedy's support for Israel. In 1969, Sirhan Sirhan was tried, convicted, and sentenced to death, a sentence later commuted to life imprisonment. As of 2011, he was still in prison in California.

Robert F. Kennedy's funeral was held at St. Patrick's Cathedral in New York, after which his body was buried at Arlington Cemetery in Virginia. A special funeral train bore his casket slowly from New York to Washington, DC. All along the route, thousands of people turned out in tribute. Paul Fusco was one of the photographers who captured images from the moving train. Many years later he wrote, "Hope-on-the-rise had again been shattered and those in most need of hope crowded the tracks of Bobby's last train, stunned into disbelief, and watched that hope trapped in a coffin pass and disappear from their lives."

It is hard to overstate the immensity of the grief and despair left in the wake of this tragedy, coming less than five years after the assassination of President Kennedy in Dallas and just two months after the murder of Dr. King. Americans were left numb and reeling from what historian Todd Gitlin, looking back on this moment, would call "violence shock." Kennedy advisor and American historian Arthur Schlesinger, delivering a commencement address in New York on June 6 as Kennedy lay dying in a Los Angeles hospital, asked,

> "What sort of people are we, we Americans? . . . We are a violent people with a violent history, and the instinct for violence has seeped into the bloodstream of our national life."

—B.H.

Young children hold signs reading "Goodbye Bobby" as Robert F. Kennedy's funeral train passes.

"I saw Kennedy's candidacy as a way in which idealism could be converted into meaningful political action, that something might be achieved to truly help those in need." —PATTI SMITH, POET AND MUSICIAN

Robert F. Kennedy's funeral train passes mourners on the way from New York City to Arlington National Cemetery.

"My brother need not be idealized, or enlarged in death beyond what he was in life; to be remembered simply as a good and decent man, who saw wrong and tried to right it, saw suffering and tried to heal it, saw war and tried to stop it . . . As he said many times, in many parts of this nation, to those he touched and sought to touch him: 'Some men see things as they are and say "why?" I dream things that never were and say "why not?"'" —FROM EDWARD M. KENNEDY'S EULOGY FOR HIS BROTHER, ROBERT

Interlude
MUSIC

MUSICALLY, 1968 was bracketed by the Summer of Love in 1967 and the Woodstock Festival in 1969, and it was as volatile and fractured a year in music as it was in the rest of society. San Francisco remained hippie central—home to bands like Jefferson Airplane, the Grateful Dead, and Big Brother and the Holding Company. John, Paul, George, and Ringo—the Beatles—had the greatest year of their careers and became true megastars. Their every move, from studying with the Maharishi Mahesh Yogi and embracing Eastern music and mysticism to beginning their Apple business ventures, was tracked that year.

A wide array of music became popular in 1968.

"Soft drugs have created far more than a chemical reaction. Even for the hundreds of thousands of kids who have not tried acid there is still a social reaction which has all the characteristics of a mind-expanding experience."
—J. MARKS, *ROCK AND OTHER FOUR-LETTER WORDS*

THE BEATLES and other musicians were open about their drug use and its influence on their music, which brought rock into the debates surrounding youth culture: free love, rebellion, political activism. Weird amalgams were being tested. The Lennon Sisters, longtime stars of Lawrence Welk's folksy TV show, left the show in 1968 in an attempt to "get groovy" with their album *Somethin' Stupid*. The hippie rock musical *Hair* debuted on Broadway in late April. The cast album, recorded in early May, sold millions of copies, and numerous covers of songs from the show reached the Top 10 over the next few years. The psychedelic sounds of the Jimi Hendrix Experience and Janis Joplin made a perfect soundtrack for the hazy, conflicted memories of the year.

The Rolling Stones' song "Street Fighting Man" was released in the United States at the end of August, a week after the violence at the Democratic National Convention in Chicago, and summed up the year's musical trends. It expressed a complex, conflicted attitude about the uprisings of the year—and it incorporated

John Lennon and Paul McCartney arrive in New York to promote their business venture, Apple Corps.

a sitar. Similarly, Big Brother and the Holding Company's version of George Gershwin's "Summertime," with Janis Joplin's raw, drawling vocal interplaying with lead guitarist James Gurley's delicate playing, summed up the general feeling that the summer of '68 had become a drag.

Although the Beatles and the Stones, Hendrix and Joplin are the artists many associate with the year, 1968 saw the full breadth of American and British music on display. It was a year where an easy listening single by a French light orchestra sold as well in America as a competing single by the Beatles, where country crossover artists like Bobby Goldsboro or Glen Campbell might play back-to-back on the radio with the heavy metal thunder of Steppenwolf, and where experiments with synthesizers, side-long tracks, and new styles like reggae and minimalism were welcomed by American consumers. It was also the year of Tiny Tim, bubblegum pop, and practically every hit released by Gary Puckett and the Union Gap. Whether we credit mind-altering drugs, *Sgt. Pepper's Lonely Hearts Club Band,* or simply the continued push by musicians and fans to explore new sonic territories, 1968 truly had it all.

Her records sold millions, but Janis Joplin was arguably more famous for her electrifying live performances.

This multiplicity was obvious to anyone who eyed those mosaic-tile Record Club advertisements in magazines in the late 1960s. As 1968 dawned, the sheer variety and creativity demonstrated by the new "pop" music led a number of people to ask serious questions about popular music's artistic value. In December of 1967, music critic Robert Christgau published an article called "Rock Lyrics Are Poetry (Maybe)" in the counterculture magazine *Cheetah*. A month later, *Rock and Other Four-Letter Words,* among the first serious books about rock music, declared, "Rock very possibly constitutes the singular, most gigantic upgrading in mass taste in world history. It has bolstered openness to expression, innovation and imagination."

"Popular music is the classical music of now."
—PAUL MCCARTNEY, MAY 1968

AS WITH MANY ARTISTIC high points, popular music in the late sixties accompanied trauma. In an era of persistent cultural anxiety punctuated by repeated tragedies, the 1968 music charts are littered with tributes to fallen heroes—Martin Luther King, Bobby Kennedy, John Coltrane, Otis Redding. Some songs, like Dion's "Abraham, Martin and John" and Otis Redding's de facto farewell song "(Sittin' On) The Dock of the Bay," left fairly indelible marks. Others, such as Arthur Conley's "Otis Sleep On" or Claudine Longet's recording of "For Bobbie (For Baby)" are largely forgotten.

45 rpm records were still the format of choice for singles in 1968.

Democratic National Convention protests. By the new year, and still prior to the release of their first album, *Kick Out the Jams,* the band landed on the cover of *Rolling Stone* magazine. That's hype.

The sound of the MC5 offers a glimpse into just how wild it felt to be in Detroit in 1968. Still recovering from week-long race riots a year earlier, the city witnessed smaller riots and a few cases of arson after the assassination of Martin Luther King. The unstable atmosphere around Detroit prompted at least one response from a major music-industry player. In 1968, Motown founder Berry Gordy Jr. took the first steps toward leaving the label's namesake city behind when he bought a house and office space in Los Angeles. In addition, Gordy faced the departure of Holland-Dozier-Holland, the label's most successful songwriting and production team, and a minor artistic rebellion as a few popular artists finally broke his unwritten rule about releasing controversial or topical songs. In spite of the apparent upheaval and the modern perception that Motown had begun its decline, during the week of Christmas 1968 Motown artists held five of the top ten spots on the Billboard Hot 100. Those songs, including "Love Child," "Cloud Nine," and Marvin Gaye's version of "I Heard It Through the Grapevine," helped redefine the Motown sound.

As the cultural tension rose, so did the volume. Where before only the words might bite, in 1968 the music itself could. Feedback, distortion, and pure aggression sprang up on rock and jazz records from the West Coast (Jimi Hendrix, Blue Cheer) to continental Europe (Peter Brötzmann's *Machine Gun*) and everywhere in between. Even the Beatles, with "Revolution" and "Helter Skelter," offered an aural assault. No band built more hype on noise, though, than Detroit's vociferous MC5. Despite only one official single, the group earned impressive reviews and a major label deal on the back of an East Coast tour opening for Cream and Big Brother and the Holding Company and gained notoriety as the only band to play in Chicago during the

"Dig me if you dare." —ARETHA FRANKLIN

ONE REASON MOTOWN seemed to be slipping might have been nothing more than the growing popularity of other black musicians. Soul music, originally centered in the black community, was more popular than ever before, increasingly bought and listened to by huge audiences of white baby boomers. Leading the charge in 1968 with eight Billboard Top 40 hits and a spot on the cover of *Time* magazine was Aretha Franklin, "the Queen of Soul." Archie Bell and the Drells ("from Houston, Texas!") hit number one with the dance "Tighten Up"; James Brown "saved" Boston and brought black empowerment to the pop chart; and both *Billboard* and *Rolling Stone* magazines named Jimi Hendrix the top artist of the year.

Country music was similarly expanding its appeal. An October issue of *Billboard* magazine called attention to the country music "hub" in Nashville with spokes that "radiate to all sections of the nation." The following month, the Country Music Association's awards show aired on national television for the first time. Though many country musicians continued to lack crossover appeal (although many were pursuing it), those that did fared well. Glen Campbell, Bobby Goldsboro, and Jeannie C. Riley each topped

ARETHA FRANKLIN

Aretha Franklin had a very good year in 1968. She was the top-selling female recording artist, with smash-hit singles like "Chain of Fools" (released the year before, but hitting the top of the charts and winning a Grammy in 1968), "Think," and "Since You've Been Gone." (She was, however, passed over for the coveted Billboard Artist of the Year award that year, in favor of the Jimi Hendrix Experience.)

Aretha gets the full *Time* cover treatment—a richly colored oil painting by Boris Chaliapin (now in the collection of the Smithsonian's National Portrait Gallery, along with most other *Time* covers) and a five-page article inside, headlined "Lady Soul." Typically *Time*'s editors strove to interpret black culture—in this case, the concept of "soul"—for their mostly white readership, though this first paragraph is cringe-inducing:

> "Has it got soul? Man, that's the question of the hour. If it has soul, then it's tough, beautiful, out of sight. It passes the test of with-itness. It has the authenticity of collard greens boiling on the stove, the sassy style of the boogaloo in a hip discotheque, the solidarity signified by 'Soul Brother' scrawled on a ghetto storefront.
>
> Soul is a way of life—but it is always the hard way . . . Soul is happening everywhere, in esthetics and anthropology, history and dietetics, haberdashery and politics."
>
> —B.H.

a *Billboard* pop chart with a single or album, and the impact of Johnny Cash's *At Folsom Prison* hardly needs to be revisited here. And consider this oddity: the song "Little Green Apples," written by country songwriter Bobby Russell, hit number two on the rhythm-and-blues chart when it was recorded by soul singer O. C. Smith, then won a Grammy for best country song. The genre was also beginning to draw interest from outside the traditional Nashville scene, most notably in the "country revival" (also known as country rock) pioneered by the Byrds, the Beau Brummels, and Bob Dylan, each of whom recorded in Music City in late 1967 or 1968.

Apart from the release of the LP *John Wesley Harding* the last week of 1967, Bob Dylan was conspicuously absent in 1968—both in his role as a popular musician and as a counterculture guide. It was the first year since 1962 that he did not release an album, and he made just one live appearance, on January 20, in a memorial concert at Carnegie Hall honoring Woody Guthrie, who had died a few months earlier. But his presence loomed over the year, so much so that by November the *Saturday Evening Post* could still call its cover-story profile of Dylan "Enter the King." Dylan, resting and recovering in Woodstock, New York, after a motorcycle accident, had not stopped writing new material. Many other artists, including the Byrds; Peter, Paul, and Mary; and Joan Baez recorded popular Dylan covers, while Jimi Hendrix took the flop Dylan single "All Along the Watchtower" and made it one of his defining records.

R&B star James Brown's big hit this year was "Say It Loud, I'm Black and I'm Proud."

JOHNNY CASH AND THE POLITICS OF THE OUTLIER

What did anyone really know about Johnny Cash's politics in 1968? Or what, for that matter, do we know now?

Cash's place in the history of 1968 was consistent with his lifelong gift for being a sort of cultural Rorschach test. While the rest of the country was focused on the war in Vietnam, the ongoing struggle for civil rights, and the fundamental challenges to law and order posed by growing unrest in America's streets, Cash was a conundrum.

He was known as the Man in Black, and there may never have been a national figure who moved so gracefully in and out of the vast gray areas of American political and cultural life without sacrificing credibility or authenticity among any of his wildly divergent audiences. Even so, Cash occupied a particularly strange and somewhat confounding place in the culture of the time.

He was first and foremost a country singer and a pure product of the South. His popularity in 1968 was largely based in patriotic, working-class enclaves. He was a staunch Christian and patriot himself, and a confidante of both Billy Graham and Richard Nixon (who was a fan). Yet he was always a bundle of contradictions, a contrarian, free-thinking anomaly in a world that increasingly embraced black-and-white extremes. Cash was always a voice for America's downtrodden, disenfranchised, and poor, yet at a time when most of the country's attention was focused on the black civil rights movement and the war, he chose to focus on the living conditions of the country's prisoners and Native Americans.

Johnny Cash's January 13 concert at Folsom Prison in Folsom, California, was released in May.

Cash was likely one of the few men in America who could be chummy with such a politically divergent cast of characters as Nixon, Graham, and Bob Dylan (he would collaborate with Dylan on "Nashville Skyline" and with Graham on a film about the life of Jesus). He would later, after a visit to Vietnam, take a clear stand against the war and would also famously refuse Nixon's Oval Office request to hear a version of Merle Haggard's anti-hippie anthem, "Okie from Muskogee."

Ever the maverick, Cash made his mark in 1968 with a recording of his legendary concerts at the Folsom State Prison in California. The album became a best seller and one of the enduring monuments of his career. Yet in the context of 1968, the Folsom Prison concerts were, like the man himself, anomalous, noticed at the time but hardly embraced by either the counterculture or the Establishment, oddly discordant with everything else that was going on in the United States. For all the passionate, politically engaged musicians and bands of the period, there were acts like the Velvet Underground, exemplars of the sorts of apolitical, decadent culture that always thrives in the shadows of larger movements of engagement in times of repression and chaos. In 1968 Andy Warhol, the Velvet Underground's champion, was painting his famous *Campbell's Soup Cans,* and, in June, he would be shot by Valerie Solanas, a disgruntled former participant in The Factory, the artist's loose-knit collaborative studio.

It is a fitting irony that 1968 brought both the birth of heavy metal (with the formation of such iconic bands as Led Zeppelin, Black Sabbath, Deep Purple, and Judas Priest) and the first stirrings of punk (in progenitors the MC5 and the Stooges), genres that would go on to mine the darker impulses, disillusionment, and disappointments of the sixties and would be embraced by a generation of largely disenfranchised and apolitical young people.

From the vantage of twenty-first-century America, Cash looks like exactly what the country needed more of in 1968: a mainstream outcast, an outlaw Christian who was open about his failings and the extent to which his faith was constantly tried, and a man willing to consider differing opinions, have his mind changed, and speak from his heart. Though he was certainly neither apolitical nor reactionary, he may have been one of the few truly righteous and politic characters on the American scene. —B.Z.

· ·

BY THE END OF THE YEAR, popular music was on the cusp of significant changes. Many icons of the hippie era were fading. The Beatles were on the verge of breaking up, Dylan was still missing, and Janis Joplin left Big Brother behind, while Buffalo Springfield and Cream had already called it quits. Yet beyond this narrow definition of "the sixties" is another world of music, one that showed the way forward. A young crop of talented women—Tammy Wynette, Dolly Parton, and Loretta Lynn—led country music into the 1970s. Wendy Carlos's *Switched-On Bach* put the Moog synthesizer and electronic music on the map. Jazz flutist Paul Horn unknowingly kicked off the new-age genre when he recorded an impromptu meditation under the dome of the Taj Mahal that focused as much on the space and spirit as it did on his instrument. Miles Davis went electric in 1968, bringing jazz fusion into the mainstream.

Across the full spectrum of styles and genres, musicians were experimenting like never before, with the support of record labels that were taking risks they would not assume today. The record-buying public had a growing knowledge of the breadth of music available and increasingly deep pockets with which to buy it. Though the true impact of the wilder forays would not be felt for a number of years, the pop charts nonetheless reflected the creative cauldron stirring just beneath the surface. In 1968 music was booming as both an industry and an art. —J.V.

TINY TIM AND THE POPULAR SPECTACLE OF THE ECCENTRIC OTHER

Tiny Tim—born Herbert Buckingham Khaury—was one of the myriad sideshows of 1968 who managed to become a household name and parlay his fifteen minutes of fame into a surprisingly enduring career as something of a cultural sideshow. The country and the culture seemed uniquely susceptible to Khaury's charms during the years from 1967 to 1971 (although he might well have thrived in a much earlier era), and he slipped through that window and worked his way into a permanent, if obscure, place in the popular consciousness and the history of the time.

Listening to recordings or watching videotape of Tiny Tim from what would have to be called his prime years, there's still something inexplicable about his celebrity credentials. Yes, he was a confirmed eccentric, probably genuine in his way. He was both sui generis and also eerily emasculated (consider just the stage name, for starters), and he was also unquestionably an encyclopedia of Tin Pan Alley and early-twentieth-century popular song. But he was relatively old by 1968 standards—he turned thirty-six that year—and had been kicking around street corners and seedy nightclubs in the Northeast for the better part of a decade before he stumbled into fame.

His persona—that of a sort of naif, an apolitical flower child—and his flamboyant get-up, quavering falsetto, and use of the ukulele marked him as a novelty act even on *Laugh-In*, the program that served as the launching pad for his stardom. In a year that didn't exactly lack colorful characters, Tiny Tim's embrace by television programmers and mainstream audiences always seemed like a token, condescending wink-wink nod to the counterculture. He was a daffy, entertaining, and utterly unthreatening representative of something he was only peripherally attached to.

In later decades, Herbert Khaury's act would have likely been merely amusing fodder for something like *The Gong Show* or, still later, a laughable outtake from *American Idol* auditions, where he surely would not have made the cut but may have had enough eccentric appeal to garner an exploitive record deal or, at the very least, become a viral celebrity via YouTube.

Scrutinized through the kaleidoscopic lens of 1968, however, the Tiny Tim phenomenon looks like just one more colorful contribution to the almost oppressive cognitive dissonance that was perhaps the year's one overweening hallmark. Oddball bit players and all manner of soft, unthreatening diversions took a bit of the sting out of a very dark year, and that Tiny Tim and "Tiptoe Through the Tulips" remain any sort of cultural touchstone over four decades later says something, surely, about the craving many, many Americans had for safe reductions of the generational weirdness that was popping up everywhere and that the average citizen couldn't—or wouldn't—quite grasp in its politicized incarnations. —B.Z.

SOUNDTRACK: 1968

Strictly in terms of sales, the Jimi Hendrix Experience was nowhere near the top of the heap in 1968. Known for its albums (four were hot sellers in 1968) and its explosive live performances, the group was not even among Billboard's Top 100 Singles Artists for the year—a list that included the Troggs (at 84), Big Brother and the Holding Company (99), Vanilla Fudge (67), Elvis Presley (56), Bobby Vinton (46), the Cowsills (20), and Archie Bell and the Drells at number 11. Number 1 was Aretha Franklin, who had eight singles in the charts that year. The sales of her albums and singles, in both the overall categories and the R&B category, were astounding.

Jimi wasn't even among the Top Male Artists, a list led by James Brown, Otis Redding, and Bobby Goldsboro (1, 2, and 3). The only Billboard best-seller list that Jimi Hendrix appeared on, in fact, was Top Album Artists, where his band ranked number 10, right behind the Beatles (7), the Doors (8), and the Monkees (9). Who was at the top of that list, in 1968, that "revolutionary" year? Herb Alpert and the Tijuana Brass, followed hard by comedian Bill Cosby, folkies Simon & Garfunkel, and country crossover artist Glen Campbell. All in all, 1968 had an amazing soundtrack. —B.H.

JULY Love It or Leave It

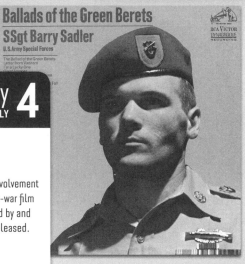

Ballads of the Green Berets
SSgt Barry Sadler
U.S. Army Special Forces

Monday 1
JULY

The United States, the Soviet Union, the United Kingdom, and many other countries sign the Nuclear Non-Proliferation Treaty at ceremonies in Washington, DC, Moscow, and London.

Thursday 4
JULY

At the height of American involvement in the Vietnam War, the pro-war film *The Green Berets*, directed by and starring John Wayne, is released.

Saturday 6
JULY

American tennis star Billie Jean King wins her third singles title at Wimbledon, her first year after turning pro.

Thursday 11
JULY

The Doors release *Waiting for the Sun*, their third studio album. The album becomes their first and only number-one album and spawns their second American number-one single, "Hello, I Love You."

Saturday **13**
JULY

The Hong Kong flu virus (H3N2) is first detected and leads to a pandemic that is eventually responsible for nearly 34,000 deaths in the United States and nearly one million deaths worldwide.

Wednesday **17**
JULY

The Arab Socialist Baath Party stages a coup in Iraq. Although initially bloodless, the so-called White Revolution becomes increasingly ruthless as a young and ambitious Saddam Hussein consolidates his power and silences his opposition.

Saturday **20**
JULY

The first Special Olympics—an athletic competition for people with developmental disabilities—opens at Chicago's Soldier Field. A key figure behind the games is Eunice Kennedy Shriver, sister of Robert and John F. Kennedy, who delivers the welcoming address.

Monday **22**
JULY

Virginia Slims cigarettes, manufactured by Philip Morris, are introduced and marketed to young professional women.

"You've come a long way, baby." —VIRGINIA SLIMS
SLOGAN, 1968

Thursday **25**
JULY

Pope Paul VI issues the encyclical *Humanae Vitae*, which reaffirms the Catholic Church's opposition to all forms of artificial contraception, including birth control pills, which had come on the market in the United States in 1960.

AIM

Sunday **28**
JULY

Members of Minneapolis's American Indian community found the American Indian Movement (AIM), which soon attracts members from across the United States and Canada.

LIFE COULD HARDLY GO ON as usual in 1968, and yet somehow, it did. There were television programs that made no mention of or reference to the war—*Bonanza* and *Gunsmoke* extended the era of the western and remained in the Nielsen Top 10—and sports from the Super Bowl to the Kentucky Derby provided a sense of continuity amidst change. A perhaps-desperate desire to preserve the illusion of continuity in American life led *Time* magazine to name "the Middle Americans" its person of the year in 1969.

MAJOR LEAGUE BASEBALL: SUCCESSFUL INTEGRATION AND THE TRIUMPH OF THE STATUS QUO

Major league baseball in 1968 provided an insulated throwback diversion from the turmoil of the times; a baseball park was perhaps the purest public refuge from the otherwise inescapable political realities of that long, violent summer.

By 1968 the sport was one of the most successfully integrated of American institutions, and many of the game's greatest black players were idolized by millions of white fans (and white, baseball card-collecting kids). Hank Aaron was in his prime, and Willie Mays was wrapping up a Hall of Fame career. That isn't to suggest that the institution was entirely colorblind, or that the black players of the era weren't subjected to the realities of America's ongoing confrontations with race, but in 1968 baseball was a remarkable bastion of relative normalcy in cities all over the country.

It was a sport whose schedule and pace lent itself to escape. Fans who couldn't make it to the ballpark could tune in to their favorite team's games on transistor radios, and the sounds of the game—at backyard barbecues, at lake cabins, in garages, or on long road trips—were a respite from the relentless flow of bad news.

The sport was also oddly—and somewhat inexplicably—insulated from the Vietnam War. Perhaps it was a testament to baseball's increasing clout as both an institution and a business, but unlike in previous wars, major league players (with very few exceptions) neither volunteered nor were drafted to serve in Vietnam.

During World War II, scores of major league players—including many of the greatest stars of the era and dozens of Hall of Famers—pulled often long stints in the military, most of them as combatants. Legends such as Ted Williams, Yogi Berra, Mickey Cochrane, Bill Dickey, Larry Doby, Bobby Doerr, Bob Feller, Stan Musial, Jackie Robinson, Duke Snider, and Warren Span all served, sometimes losing years in the prime of their careers.

By 1968, however, only a handful of major leaguers (and not a single star player among them) was sent to Vietnam, and only one—Roy Gleason—was wounded. —B.Z.

While the presidential contest was the most closely watched this year, other victories, such as this high school basketball All-Conference trophy, were also hotly pursued.

By July many Americans saw baseball as a respite from the upheaval of the year. On the diamond, clean-cut young men enacted centuries-old rituals of masculinity in a sport with a gift for self-mythologizing that rivaled even Richard Nixon's. Most teams banned facial hair and regulated players' hair length well into the 1970s (the New York Yankees, famously, still do). And, unlike American college students, players were happy to submit for the privilege of playing professionally. The A's, formerly of Kansas City, played their first season in Oakland, California, providing a different notoriety to the city the Black Panthers called home. On the field, black, white, Latino, and Native American players worked together seamlessly, seemingly unaffected by the deep divisions that were becoming apparent in civil society. The All-Star Game, played on July 9, was the first held indoors, in a new setting (the Houston Astrodome) that seemed to hold further promise of American mastery over nature.

The year is known as the Year of the Pitcher, a time when pitching held the strongest advantage over hitting since the early 1900s. St. Louis Cardinal Bob Gibson set a single-season record for lowest earned run average—1.12—that still stands; Los Angeles Dodger Don Drysdale set a record by pitching fifty-eight consecutive scoreless innings, and Carl Yastrzemski of the Boston Red Sox led the league in hitting with a .301 batting average, still the lowest for a league leader in hitting since the dead-ball era of the early 1900s. The domination of hitters by pitchers was quickly corrected by rule changes that went into effect in the 1969 season. Similarly, baseball commissioner Bowie Kuhn imposed further order and structure on the expanding sport by developing eastern and western divisions within the American and National Leagues.

By October, when the *Sports Illustrated* cover below appeared, the St. Louis Cardinals had repeated their 1967 domination of the National League and were battling the American League's Detroit Tigers in the World Series. Despite *Sports Illustrated*'s claims, the Cardinals would end up losing three games straight to allow the Tigers to take the title. But history remembers the 1968 Cardinals' stable of stars kindly: a surprising number of these players are now in the Hall of Fame or well known for other reasons.

Manager Red Schoendienst, a Hall of Fame Cardinals player in his own right, is pictured

The St. Louis Cardinals, defending champions, appeared on the cover of *Sports Illustrated* the same week they lost the World Series to the Detroit Tigers.

in the *SI* cover photo, and the accompanying article lauds his skills as manager and the respect his players have for him. Also pictured are three future Hall of Fame players: Bob Gibson, perhaps the most dominating and domineering pitcher of the year—and the decade; Lou Brock, the speedy left fielder who held the career stolen base record for two decades; and power-hitting first baseman Orlando Cepeda, the first Puerto Rican player to start in an All-Star Game. Others pictured are well known for other reasons: at left is right fielder Roger Maris, whose career was cut short by injuries but in 1961 had broken Babe Ruth's single-season home run record by hitting sixty-one homers in a season. Tim McCarver, seated at Maris's right, would go on to a long career in national baseball broadcasting. Curt Flood, seated third from the back, was perhaps the best all-around centerfielder in the game and may have been a Hall of Fame player but would sacrifice the end of his career by suing Major League Baseball to help repeal baseball's reserve clause, which bound players to teams in perpetuity. Though Flood lost his lawsuit, some of the best years of his playing career, and the respect and friendship of many of his colleagues, he was vindicated by history as his actions shepherded in the era of free agency—another legacy of the 1960s commitment to self-expression and freedom (and commerce). —E.A.

"The whole thing is a mess. The sooner we get the hell out of there the better. But what bothers me about the peace crowd is that you can tell from their attitude, the way they look and what they say, that they don't really love this country. Some of them seem *glad* to have a chance to criticize us . . . To hell with them! Let them get out, leave, if they don't like it here! My son didn't die so they can look filthy and talk filthy and insult everything we believe in and everyone in the country—me and my wife and people here on the street, and the next street, and all over." —FATHER OF A SOLDIER KILLED IN VIETNAM, TO ROBERT COLES, *THE MIDDLE AMERICANS*, 1971

. . . .

ROD MCKUEN AND THE POETRY OF 1968

It's curious (but not terribly surprising) that other than the mostly a-poetical antics of Allen Ginsberg and the occasional odd mention of poet Robert Lowell's appearances on the campaign trail with Eugene McCarthy, poets get short shrift in most of the histories of 1968.

It was a golden age of American poetry, really, and there has arguably never been a time when poets were so politically engaged—in both their work and their lives—in social movements and public dissent. Many of the great twentieth-century legends were still alive in 1968, many still working at the height of their powers, and a large number of the enduring voices of the next four decades were just emerging or hitting their stride. Small literary journals and magazines were flourishing and full of lively and topical stuff. New York City launched a popular, if short lived, Dial-A-Poem service. Many of the leading musical voices of the time—Bob Dylan, obviously, but also Leonard Cohen, Paul Simon, and myriad other folkies—were being embraced as poets by a generation of young admirers. Even Eugene McCarthy, the Democratic nominee for president, was a published poet. Two of his poems appeared in the April 12, 1968, issue of *Life* magazine. Yet, as has always been the case (at least since Robert Frost's long run as both a legitimate talent and a minor national icon), the poets of 1968 were largely ignored even in the general population. Ginsberg, of course, was a notable (and colorful) exception, but he was something of a Beat interloper who'd somewhat awkwardly embraced the spiritual and sartorial trappings of the new counterculture, and he was by then known as much for his daffy persona and eccentric celebrity as he was for anything he was writing at the time.

All of this, though, begs the question: how does any cultural history of that year or that decade account for the wild success of Rod McKuen, the decidedly light and mellow ruminative poet who placed three volumes of "verse" on the best seller lists in 1968? McKuen's work was at least typeset and marketed as poetry, and titles such as *Listen to the Warm* and *Stanyan Street and Other Sorrows* certainly sounded vaguely poetic. The poems themselves could be almost simultaneously oblique and transparent, but they were unquestionably about *feelings*—"groovy" feelings, it's fair to say—and had a sort of flyweight heaviness to them.

McKuen was maybe slightly trippy, but he was also soft headed and safe, a sixties holdover from the bachelor-pad embrace of the earlier Beat lifestyle, without any of the Beat's real philosophy or commitment. As such he was something of a come-on artist—perhaps the one area where he most approached a sort of poetic authenticity—and he was unquestionably 1968's chief poet of the half-hearted embrace. His books were perfect graduation gifts from befuddled parents and square friends for kids who were presumed to be somehow "with it."

For decades after his peak, McKuen's books would become the sort of cultural milfoil that clogged the shelves of America's used bookstores and thrift shops, but he was not without a slight (and slightly dubious) legacy as a pop poetry progenitor: kitsch historians might note that his work paved the way for Richard Bach (*Jonathan Livingston Seagull*), Susan Polis Schutz (founder of the Blue Mountain online card company), and scores of other earnest composers of gossamer verse that was ready-made for greeting cards. —B.Z.

NOT EVERYONE WAS FEELING the extreme passions of right or left in 1968, but the polarizations of the year lent themselves to a "with us or against us" outlook that enabled Democratic party leaders to warn primary voters that a vote for McCarthy would be celebrated in Hanoi. Similarly, a desire to assert themselves against an elite establishment brought supporters into line with avowed segregationist George Wallace, who famously stated at the conclusion of his American Independent Party campaign, "They've looked down their nose at you and me a long time. They've called us rednecks—the Republicans and the Democrats. Well, we're going to show Mr. Nixon and Mr. Humphrey, there sure are still a lot of rednecks in this country."

Wallace solidified the alliance between the desire to turn back the clock on civil rights and the unapologetic use of force in Vietnam and at home—racism and the law-and-order crowd—when he named General Curtis LeMay as his running mate in October. Despite Wallace's appeals to "rednecks," he spoke to capacity crowds across working-class white areas throughout the summer and fall. It's tempting to say that Wallace "only" won the Deep South (Arkansas, Louisiana, Mississippi, Alabama, and Georgia), but his electoral showing was the best for a third-party candidate since Theodore Roosevelt, and no third-party candidate has even come close since then. —E.A.

. . . .

GEORGE WALLACE AND LESTER MADDOX AND THE POPULIST INSURGENCE

In a year of attacks and counterattacks, actions and reactions, there was arguably no assault on the American political system more strange or unexpected—and perhaps none with more lasting consequences—than the unruly populist one-two punch that reared up out of the South in the form of George Wallace and Lester Maddox.

Pundits at the time might have been inclined to dismiss Wallace and Maddox as aberrations and archetypes of the bumptious bumpkin—which to some extent they certainly were; both men were reliable sources of appalling utterances—but while their ascent may have represented a troubling deviation, it was also a very real symptom of a roiling unrest that was brewing in the peripheries and

far-flung working class penumbrae that have always served as a sort of petri dish for the most hostile impulses of populism.

Wallace, of course, was a calculating career politico, an old-school Southern Democrat who had been running for one office or another in Georgia since the 1940s. In the wake of civil rights legislation and incursions from Washington on states' rights, he had, in his initial gubernatorial campaign, made the decision to dig in his heels on segregation and relish his role as the angry outsider and the voice for disenfranchised whites.

It proved to be an effective strategy at the time. Wallace probably understood better than almost anyone else in America what he was up to, and the full extent of the sense of futility and helplessness and frustration that was mounting in quiet places nationwide. By 1968, when Wallace launched his third-party candidacy for the presidency, those feelings were surfacing all over the country, and in places far from the South.

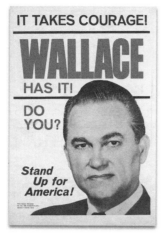

Norman Mailer's *Miami and the Siege of Chicago* is one account of the 1968 political year. After attending a poorly organized Black Power event, he writes, "the reporter became aware of a peculiar emotion in himself, for he had not ever felt it consciously before. It was a simple emotion and very unpleasant to him—he was tired of negroes and their rights. If he felt even a hint this way, then what immeasurable tides of rage must be loose in America?"

Wallace—and, to a much lesser extent, Maddox—tapped into those immeasurable tides. Both men were purely of the South, but Wallace was perhaps more a product of the system, while Maddox, an amateur bicycle racer and the owner of a fried-chicken restaurant, was more a product of the

ABOVE: Wallace's "courage" tapped into resentments felt by working-class and poor whites. RIGHT: Like George Wallace, Georgia governor Lester Maddox was a proponent of segregation; Maddox was also famous for carrying a "Wake Up America" alarm clock around with him, for claiming he refused to serve African Americans in his restaurant, and for opposing a day of mourning in Atlanta for Dr. Martin Luther King Jr.'s funeral.

culture. He had made his name by refusing to serve blacks in his restaurant and, despite having none of Wallace's political savvy or organizational skills, somehow managed, in 1966, to bumble his way into the Georgia governor's office (after surviving one of the most chaotic run-off elections in American history).

Maddox served an undistinguished and often confounding term as governor, but that didn't deter him from making his own run at the Democratic presidential nomination in 1968. His candidacy went nowhere, and while he was ultimately a less virulent and influential figure than Wallace (who won five states in '68—all in the South—and garnered almost ten million votes), the legacy of both men is very much alive in American politics. They opened doors all over the country for outsider, anti-Washington, fiercely anti-intellectual and anti-institutional candidates for offices at both the state and national levels. —B.Z.

AUGUST "Welcome to Chicago"

Monday 5
AUGUST

Ronald Reagan announces his candidacy for the presidency on the opening day of the Republican National Convention in Miami Beach.

Thursday 8
AUGUST

Richard M. Nixon is nominated for president on the first ballot at the Republican National Convention, beating out California governor Ronald Reagan and New York governor Nelson Rockefeller. Later that day, Nixon chooses Maryland governor Spiro Agnew as his running mate.

Wednesday 7
AUGUST

James Brown, the top-selling male musician of 1968, records "Say It Loud, I'm Black and I'm Proud." The funk song becomes one of the most popular Black Power anthems of the 1960s.

Monday 12
AUGUST

Big Brother and the Holding Company release *Cheap Thrills*, their second studio album and the last with Janis Joplin. The album reaches Number 1 on the Billboard charts in its eighth week and by the end of the year is the most successful album of 1968, having sold nearly one million copies.

Monday 19
AUGUST

Tom Wolfe releases two books on the same day: *The Pump House Gang* and *The Electric Kool-Aid Acid Test*, a wild, drug-fueled romp with novelist Ken Kesey and his Merry Pranksters on a "psychedelic" painted bus.

"The world was simply and sheerly divided into 'the aware,' those who had the experience of being vessels of the divine, and a great mass of 'the unaware,' 'the unmusical,' 'the unattuned.' Or: you're either on the bus, or off the bus." —TOM WOLFE, *THE ELECTRIC KOOL-AID ACID TEST*

Tuesday 20
AUGUST

Forces from the Soviet Union and other Eastern-bloc nations invade Czechoslovakia to halt the political liberalization known as Prague Spring. Approximately 500 Czechs and Slovaks are wounded and 108 are killed in the invasion.

Saturday 24
AUGUST

France—since 1960 a member of the club of nations with nuclear weapons—explodes its first thermonuclear bomb over an atoll in Polynesia, a 2.6-megaton blast.

Wednesday 28
AUGUST

Tammy Wynette records her hit single "Stand By Your Man."

Monday 26
AUGUST

The Democratic National Convention opens in Chicago. In the days that follow, thousands of demonstrators take to the streets to protest the Vietnam War. Violent clashes occur between protesters and police.

Thursday 29
AUGUST

Vice President Hubert H. Humphrey is nominated by the Democrats as their candidate for the presidency, defeating Senators Eugene McCarthy and George McGovern.

Humphrey partisans were some of the few who looked optimistically toward Chicago.

IT IS IMPOSSIBLE TO OVERSTATE the intensity of the anxiety that gripped the country in the months leading up to the Democrats' convention in late August. Beginning as early as January 1968, organized groups of the "New Left" were calling for an "Election Year Offensive," for opponents of the Vietnam War to gather in Chicago to press their demands

"Chicago—the movement's irresistible force collided with Mayor Daley's immovable object, while the television cameras floodlit the clash into national theater . . . It was as if everyone were playing out a fantasy version of Vietnam: act tough, try to intimidate, win over the center with a show of force, draw the other side into acting every bit as monstrous as you said it was." — TODD GITLIN, *THE SIXTIES: YEARS OF HOPE, DAYS OF RAGE*

Military police vehicles covered in barbed wire prepared for the 1968 Democratic National Convention. Some 12,000 police, 5,000 soldiers, and 6,000 National Guardsmen were on duty in Chicago for the DNC.

Democrats may have been welcome in Chicago, but by August national organizers were urging protesters to stay away; as a result, only about 10,000 came.

for an end to the war, or at least for the Democrats to include a "peace plank" into the platform that was going to be adopted at the convention. The newly formed anarchic Yippie organization announced that they would be there, too, holding a deliberately outrageous and provocative "Festival of Life."

Meanwhile in Chicago, the city's combative and belligerent "Mayor for Life" Richard J. Daley was vowing to negate—with force—any action by any "hippie" who dared to show up. The Chicago police, still deeply shaken by the deadly rioting on the city's West Side in April after King's assassination, braced for a battle.

And the battles came. First in the city's Lincoln Park, where police used tear gas to clear out protesters camping in the park, then even more brutally a few nights later, in Grant Park downtown. Bloodied protesters chanted for the ubiquitous TV cameras: "The whole world is watching!" (The whole world *was,* it seems, watching, but, conversely, Americans were also watching what was going on thousands of miles away, in Czechoslovakia, where Soviet tanks and helmeted troops were violently suppressing the liberalization movement known as "Prague Spring.")

Inside the Chicago convention hall several miles away, there were other battles—over rules, over planks in the platform, over candidates. In the end, the antiwar plank was defeated, along with peace candidates George

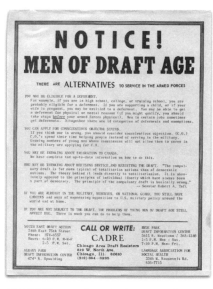

CADRE (Chicago Area Draft Resisters) provided advice and assistance to young men wishing to illegally avoid the draft; they also organized antiwar protests.

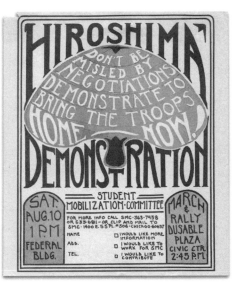

The Student Mobilization Committee coordinated demonstrations with the Mobe—the National Mobilization Committee—in Chicago; their primary goal was to try to turn public opinion against the war. Here they did so by playing into nuclear fears.

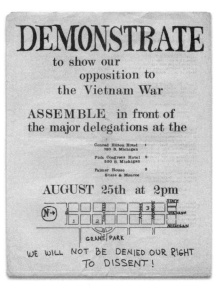

Because the convention activities were held almost a mile from downtown Chicago, much of the protest activity happened near the official conference hotel, the Chicago Hilton ("1" on the map in this flyer).

"At Joe the Bartender's in the Hilton Plaza . . . where the Nixon people came to celebrate, the kids were out, the Young Republicans and the Youth for American Freedom, a table or two of the audience so much as the mood . . . There was slyness in the air, and patience, confidence of the win—a mood was building which could rise to a wave . . . There would be talk of new order before too long."

—NORMAN MAILER, *MIAMI AND THE SIEGE OF CHICAGO*

Peaceful protestors in front of the Hilton during the Democratic National Convention in Chicago.

McGovern (standing in for the assassinated Robert Kennedy) and Eugene McCarthy. Vice President Hubert H. Humphrey, though damaged by his support for the war and by the violence on the streets, emerged the nominee.

Little hint of the violence that was to come in Chicago at the end of the month had been provided by the Republican convention held in Miami Beach on August 5–8. The city was largely spared the demonstrations that crippled the Democrats—not because the Re-

publicans were in any way the "peace party" but because they were not the party in power and thus bore little responsibility for the prosecution of the Vietnam War. Still, during the convention there were several days of rioting across the bay in Miami's Liberty City community, an impoverished area long known as "Colored Town."

The convention itself was also undramatic. Governors Nelson Rockefeller and Ronald Reagan (who only officially announced

THE CAMPAIGNERS

The 1968 election engendered a great deal of obvious tension in white Middle America, and it was plenty apparent that this was an election not about personalities but about politics on a very black-and-white (literally and metaphorically) level. It featured a cast of unappealing candidates and had a transparently glum and cynical quality that seemed to feed the country's political disaffection.

It didn't appear to matter what side anyone was on that November; there was a palpable despair and disgust on both sides of the political fence and a sense of profound civic exhaustion. It showed up in virtually every account of the year's campaigns and conventions, even in the dispatches that weren't from the burgeoning gonzo fringe of the Fourth Estate.

King and Kennedy were dead by the time the conventions rolled around; mass demonstrations all over the country had been stymied or crushed; Johnson had abdicated without much explanation;

the war was still raging every night on television (and in the mountains and jungles and cities of a country that few Americans could find on a map). In the wake of so much discord and dissent, the presidential campaign ultimately amounted to a stubborn status quo repudiation of the major events of the year, a sort of glum assertion of historical inevitability that helped to spawn a generation of shruggers and cynics. —B.Z.

Delegate Donald Fraser of Minnesota wore this badge to access official convention events.

his candidacy when he landed in Miami for the start of the proceedings) offered little challenge to front-runner Richard Nixon, who won handily on the first ballot. Nixon chose Maryland governor Spiro Agnew as his running mate, and the ticket went on to defeat the Democrats and George Wallace

in November. Nixon's acceptance speech on August 8 was perhaps the greatest rhetorical moment of his career—a soaring series of inspirational stories. No one, of course, could have predicted that exactly six years later, on August 8, 1974, Richard Nixon would resign from the presidency in disgrace.

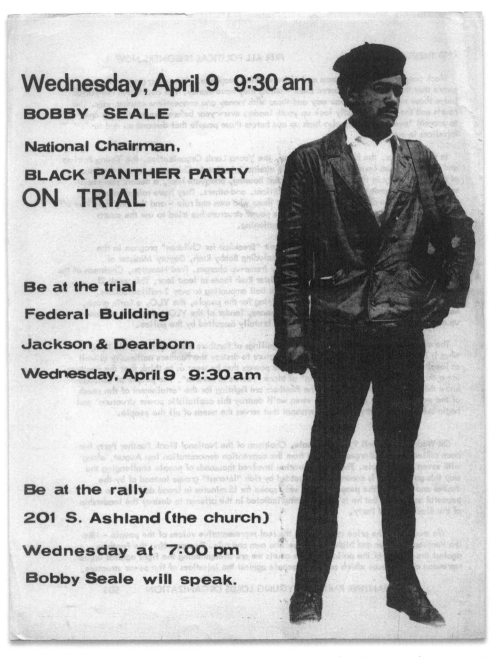

After the Democratic National Convention, Bobby Seale and seven others (the Chicago Eight) were charged with conspiracy and inciting to riot.

PRAGUE, AUGUST 1968

When Soviet tanks, accompanied by 200,000 Warsaw Pact troops, rolled into Prague on August 21, 1968, the long experiment in political liberalization known as Prague Spring was finally over. Inaugurated with Slovak Alexander Dubcek's accession to leadership of the Czechoslovakian Communist Party in January of 1968, Prague Spring came to full flower with the April 5 publication of an Action Program laying out hopes for "socialism with a human face." Dubcek did not seek to overthrow Communist rule but rather to liberalize it—to decentralize the economy, allow greater freedom of the press, reduce secret police surveillance, produce more consumer goods, and, above all, to create "a unique experiment in democratic communism."

On June 26, 1968, censorship was abolished and anti-Soviet opinions were printed in the Prague newspapers—unheard-of in Communist countries. The Action Program also allowed Czechoslovakians (who could afford it) to travel internationally and set in motion plans to divide the country into separate Czech and Slovak republics that better fit the ethnic groups' disparate histories.

While most Czechoslovakians seemed to welcome the reforms, some high-ranking party officials had second thoughts about moving away from the safety of the Soviet Union. Though the Action Program was focused on expanding domestic freedoms, and in fact reiterated the importance of remaining part of the Warsaw Pact, Soviet leadership also saw much to fear in these reforms, particularly if they were to spread to other Communist republics. Party leaders met with Dubcek as early as March to urge him to contain the Czechoslovakian media and youth, the primary sources of the drive for liberalization. In his autobiography, *Hope Dies Last*, Dubcek recalls that he was chastised for "losing control" over the situation and for "permitting a diversity of opinion that, in their view, bordered on 'counterrevolution.'"

Dubcek refused to back down from April's Action Program and continued to argue that his efforts were increasing the popularity of Communism among his citizens, not threatening stability. Leonid Brezhnev disagreed and began developing a doctrine that limited the sovereignty of states in the Warsaw Pact. It was issued in November to retroactively justify the invasion of Czechoslovakia.

Knowing there was no way Czechoslovakia could effectively resist the invasion and hoping to avoid civilian deaths, Dubcek urged his citizens to welcome the Soviet troops nonviolently, and for the most part they did. One last gasp of Prague Spring was felt as Czechoslovakians painted over street signs and attempted to argue with invading troops or greet them with flowers, but by the end of the month, censorship had been reinstated and the Action Program declared invalid. Internationally, this show of Soviet aggression undermined antiwar protests and gave credence to the hawkish view that maintained the necessity of a hard-line anti-Communist stance. —E.A.

SEPTEMBER Sisterhood Is Powerful

Friday 6
SEPTEMBER

Outside the Miss America pageant on the Atlantic City boardwalk, feminist protesters crown a live sheep Miss America and toss "instruments of female torture," such as bras, girdles, false eyelashes, and hair curlers, into a Freedom Trash Can.

"We're protesting because the beauty of the black woman has been ignored. It hasn't been respected. We'll show black beauty for public consumption—herald her beauty and applaud it." —J. MORRIS ANDERSON, FOUNDER, MISS BLACK AMERICA

Tuesday 3
SEPTEMBER

Beat novelist Jack Kerouac appears as a guest on conservative pundit William F. Buckley's television show *Firing Line* and joins a panel discussion on "the Hippies."

Sunday 8
SEPTEMBER

Saundra Williams of Philadelphia is crowned the first Miss Black America at a pageant designed as a counter-event to the traditional (and white-dominated) Miss America contest.

•

Huey Newton, the Black Panther Party minister of defense, who had been charged with first-degree murder, assault, and kidnapping for his confrontation with an Oakland police officer in October 1967, is found guilty of voluntary manslaughter.

•

In Warsaw, Poland, Ryszard Siwiec, an accountant and teacher, sets himself on fire in front of 100,000 spectators at a harvest festival in protest of the recent Soviet invasion of Czechoslovakia. He dies four days later.

Monday 9
SEPTEMBER

Arthur Ashe wins the U.S. Open—the first African American man to win one of tennis's Grand Slam tournaments.

Thursday 19
SEPTEMBER

Funny Girl, the film version of the hit Broadway musical based on the life of entertainer Fanny Brice, debuts in New York and goes on to become the highest-grossing movie of 1968.

Tuesday 24
SEPTEMBER

60 Minutes, described as "a kind of magazine for television," debuts on CBS. The first edition goes inside the campaign headquarters of presidential candidates Nixon and Humphrey and also features clips from the Oscar-winning documentary *Why Man Creates*.

Monday 30
SEPTEMBER

Bull Tales, a comic strip by Yale student Garry Trudeau, makes its debut in the *Yale Daily News*, satirizing campus life. When it goes into syndication two years later, it is renamed *Doonesbury*.

•

The first Boeing 747 jumbo jet rolls out of the company's new factory in Everett, Washington. With a wingspan of 196 feet, the 747 is more than twice the size of the largest jets in service.

"What the women's movement did was name a set of contradictions that were being experienced by millions of women . . . All you had to do was name it, and women were ready to act. Something they had felt and been frustrated by and felt alone with suddenly had a label and you weren't alone, and you could talk to other people about it, and together you could act to change it. So for a while there, it was like a wildfire; it just exploded across the country." —SARA EVANS, HISTORIAN, ORAL HISTORY INTERVIEW

ACROSS THE NATION, women's roles were in a curious flux. Young women were moving in with their boyfriends, causing scandal nationwide, yet they were more concerned with freedom and civil liberties than with sex. Advertisements and consumer culture praised the beautiful, soft-spoken woman, but feminists from across the country loudly protested the iconic Miss America pageant. Career women were more often than not confined to secretarial roles, yet new television shows and remarkable female athletes reflected a changing landscape. From the first women's march for peace in Washington, DC, in January to the first national women's liberation conference in November, "second-wave" feminism coalesced in 1968.

"Every girl in this world should know how to dance beautifully, how to flirt successfully, how to make love divinely—and how to make crepes."
—PAT MONTANDON, *HOW TO BE A PARTY GIRL*, 1968

ALTHOUGH 1968 SAW many challenges to core values in American society, discussions on the roles of women were still uncommon. In the mainstream, women had traditional roles, mores, and goals. The pride and power that a mainstream woman commanded were supposed to derive from her beauty, poise, and successful home.

"Even though many women did work outside the home in many kinds of jobs, the assumption was that they didn't need to work, they weren't supposed to be supporting families, they shouldn't have aspirations and ambitions for work outside the home. Their identities were supposed to be completely rooted in the roles of wife and mother. Mostly I think girls imagined their adult lives in terms of, 'What kind of man would I be married to?' Because that's where your identity came from. Would you want to be married to a doctor or a lawyer, or perhaps a minister, you know, because there were roles for the wives of all of those . . . It was not uncommon for a woman to say 'we' went to graduate school, meaning he went to graduate school and she supported him. And as soon as he was done, her life became wife of that profession, and caretaker of the home." —SARA EVANS

ABOVE: Traditional gender roles persisted in liberal politics.

BY 1968, RACIALLY DIVIDED Help Wanted ads in newspapers had been banned, but the ban did not extend to gender. Jobs in the Female column were often temporary by nature, as there was enormous pressure on a newly married woman to leave the workforce. Married women of a certain class were expected to be wholly supportive of their husbands' careers, and this notion was rarely challenged even by the most vocal members of the New Left movements. Masculinity continued to be defined as the ability to provide for a family; the presence of a working wife might suggest that a man was not performing his role properly. While many blue-collar and minority men sought jobs that would enable them to become their family's sole breadwinner, such jobs could be hard to come by; thus, many working-class women and women of color sought precisely the privilege middle-class white women found so oppressive: the ability to not work. What bound these two groups together, regardless of color or class, was the dearth of options for working women and the lack of respect for their labor.

For the most part the jobs open to women were limited to a few traditionally female careers: teaching, service, and office support. A woman seeking a glamorous job could become an airline stewardess, and a woman seeking a well-respected job could become a secretary. Although her role was supportive, a secretary did need to master a set of unique skills to succeed, and there was a certain degree of respect for women who did the job well. Typewriters like the Selectric, a staple in any

Reporter Sherrie Mazingo works on a story for the *Minneapolis Tribune;* women could get jobs at newspapers, but their path wasn't easy, and they were often limited to "domestic" beats.

office, were almost exclusively operated by young women.

Women's career options were changing by 1968; however, many felt that those changes came too slowly and with difficulty. A decade-long fight to remove the age and marital restriction on airline stewardesses was won only three weeks before the Miss America protests in Atlantic City. Muriel Siebert became the first woman to hold a seat on the New York Stock Exchange in 1968, and incredibly, for the first time, women in the state of Mississippi were able to sit on juries.

"She has prominently affected the way 50 percent of society thinks and feels about itself in the vast area of physical exercise . . . she has made a whole sport boom because of the singular force of her presence." —FRANK DEFORD, "MRS. BILLIE JEAN KING!" *SPORTS ILLUSTRATED*, MAY 19, 1975

DESPITE STILL-LIMITED career choices, America's most visible female role models were branching out. In sports, two very different women took center stage. Peggy Fleming embodied all that seemed right about America as she won the gold medal in figure skating at the Winter Olympics in Grenoble, France. Billie Jean King, a vocal advocate for the rights of marginalized people, won her third singles title at Wimbledon but received only half of what the men's champion was awarded. King was inspired to seek equality in her sport, changing the structure of women's tennis and securing equal pay for male and female tennis players at the U.S. Open and other tennis tournaments (though Wimbledon would not establish equal men's and women's prizes until 2007). Ironically, her success gave Virginia Slims an opportunity to back up its quasi-feminist sloganeering by sponsoring what would become the Women's Tennis Association Tour.

Billie Jean King hitting a backhand at Wimbledon, wearing her signature cat-eye glasses.

Though the Pope issued an official position against it in July, many saw birth control as fundamental to women's freedom.

"The media kept saying, 'Well, this is about sex.' Or, 'Aren't you ever going to get married?' And it's not really even about marriage; it's about choices, it's about women having choices. And actually, I think really, that's much scarier."
—GRACE LECLAIR, ORAL HISTORY INTERVIEW

GRACE LINDA LECLAIR was a reluctant spokeswoman for the women's movement, involuntarily becoming a champion for co-habitating co-eds nationwide when her living arrangements were revealed in an article in the *New York Times* on March 4, 1968. The advent of oral contraceptives in 1960 had changed the sexual landscape, making it possible for women to be sexually active without the risk of pregnancy. This reorientation of sex away from reproduction and toward pleasure caused scandal, particularly as young middle- and upper-class women and men began to cohabitate outside of marriage.

When Barnard College expelled LeClair for living with her long-term boyfriend off campus, she brought a lawsuit against them. Although she received hate mail calling her a whore and telling her that she would rot in hell, she was also keenly aware that sexual deviance was not at the heart of the nation's mortification. For LeClair and for many others, the conversation about sex was only the surface of the real issue in gender and relationship roles. At its heart was a discussion about women's power, women's freedom, and women's civil liberties.

Ironically, women who joined social justice movements often faced the contradictions of normative gender roles, perhaps even more so than women in the mainstream. For some men, the "sexual revolution" meant unfettered access to the bodies of liberated women rather than greater equality and respect in gender relations.

RESPECTABLE RADICALS?

Women are always present in histories of political movements in the United States, but feminism is not. Movements politicizing the category of "woman" arose intermittently in the first two hundred years of U.S. history and often stemmed from women's participation in other social movements. Historically, women often drew on the widely accepted *differences* between the sexes to argue that their roles as mothers, which naturally afforded them a great deal of influence in shaping the next generation, should also afford them increased political power.

Much feminist activism was limited to middle-class white women, who drew on their presumed "respectability" and sought to impart it onto working-class women or women of color, creating an unequal sisterhood. Some also used their racial and class privilege as planks in their arguments for rights: for example, after the Civil War, Southern white women argued for woman suffrage to counterbalance the votes of newly enfranchised black men. The feminist movement was not always inclusive of or appealing to poor women and women of color. When such women were active in other arenas, they often did not identify themselves primarily as women.

By the 1960s, however, women were coming together to politicize the category of womanhood and denaturalize gender-based inequality. Second-wave feminists (as they came to be known) attempted to establish *equality* and *gender-neutrality* as important categories. American women were acquiring increased legal protections throughout the 1960s as first the Equal Pay Act (1963) and then the Civil Rights Act of 1964 established sex as a protected category in the workplace, though domestic workers, primarily women, continued to be excluded from these protections. Old Left activists of the 1930s joined a new generation active in antiwar and civil rights movements and baby boomers reacting against the unhappiness they witnessed in their middle-class mothers.

These mothers, trained for professional lives and then confined to roles as homemakers, were the ones Smith College alumna Betty Friedan wrote about in 1963's *The Feminine Mystique*. Friedan's book was only part of heightened feminist consciousness in the postwar era, which arguably began a full decade earlier when Simone de Beauvoir's *The Second Sex* appeared in English. Three years prior to Friedan's book, the arrival of hormonal contraception established sexuality as a site of pleasure and self-exploration. Technically, though, the Pill was still primarily prescribed to married women who wished to control their fertility, and its development proceeded in violation of the rights of many Puerto Rican women, on whom it was tested without their consent.

Second-wave feminists also organized, forming two of the most enduring and mainstream feminist organizations: National Organization for Women and the National Abortion Rights and Action League (now known as NARAL Pro-Choice America). More radical platforms contributed to the formation of these groups and were in constant conversation with them. As conservative pushback painted the liberal, rights-seeking framework of NOW and NARAL as radical, truly radical groups and demands that were at the core of the movement in 1968 were marginalized. —E.A.

"For young men it's directly a generational revolt: our fathers and the structures they built, whether it's military or university rules, or the corporate world—they aren't doing it right. We want to replace them and do it better. For young women to rebel against the power of the fathers is basically to step outside of a set of prescribed roles: what they're supposed to be and how they're supposed to behave, and what they're supposed to do, and what they can imagine becoming. It's really different for them. And so they start breaking gender rules.

"The young men I don't think so much break with the idea of what a man is . . . They aren't thinking that they're going to redo the relationship between women and men, they're just going to prove their manhood in a different way. Whereas women's revolt necessarily required them to rethink the relationship between men and women and what kind of power they're going to have vis-à-vis their peers . . . not just their fathers. And so in all of these movements, women step out of their prescribed roles, discover new capacities, and then find that their male comrades are saying: Wait a minute; you're not supposed to be doing that."

—SARA EVANS, ORAL HISTORY INTERVIEW

THE LIMITS THEY came up against in so many different sectors of society brought women together. They formed women's liberation groups and participated in consciousness-raising movements, embracing the idea that "the personal is political." They argued that the dissatisfactions they experienced in their personal and professional lives were not the results of their own shortcomings but rather a result of structural, systemic injustice.

Women had made strides in illuminating the possibilities life could hold for them. At the same time, though, many of the advertisements, products, and entertainment directed at women from popular culture sought to limit these options. Virginia Slims cigarettes capitalized on the passion women's liberation had aroused by tying its product to liberation, assuring modern women they had "come a

Senator Walter Mondale crowns Donna Clemings as Bemidji State University's homecoming queen. Some saw the yearly ritual as empowering, while others felt it was sexist.

long way, baby." Items like curlers, false eyelashes, and girdles continued to be sold as essential objects in a woman's repertoire. Although the sexual revolution was occurring on campuses and in counterculture communities, many women in the mainstream were active participants in a consumerist culture that had a clear picture of what it expected them to be. Women across the nation competed in contests where they were selected for their poise, beauty, and success in embodying traditional femininity. Winning such contests earned young women respect and attention and was certainly one way to access power, but such victories also glorified a very narrow set of values, and the winners were almost always middle class, white, and hoping to pursue a life of gracious homemaking.

By 1968, women across ideological lines could agree that the objectification of women was a problem. Conservatives tried to make this problem into one of liberated women's own making, arguing that their sexual freedom had caused women to objectify themselves. San Francisco's most famous hostess and socialite Pat Montandon, assuring her readers that "all normal girls want to be sexy," nevertheless claimed that "there isn't a person on earth . . . who wants to be thought of as a sex object." She provided a simple solution, however: "If you can give a man comfort, beauty, and warmth as a hostess in your own home, then he will consider your worth as a person, rather than seeing you just as a sex object."

Some women's liberation protestors, however, had a very different idea for countering objectification. They identified the Miss America pageant, nationally televised every September from its home in Atlantic City, New Jersey, as one of the most overt sites of women's objectification, and they set out to end it. Miss America was under attack on other fronts in 1968 as well. In response to the pageant's exclusion of women of color, a Philadelphia entrepreneur began a Miss Black America contest in Atlantic City. While Miss Black America continued to judge women on their appearance and conformity to a narrow set of standards, recognizing the beauty and intelligence of black women as qualities worth celebrating was in keeping with the Black Power spirit of the times.

"Miss America represents what women are supposed to be: inoffensive, bland, apolitical. If you are tall, short, over or under what weight The Man prescribes you should be, forget it. Personality, articulateness, intelligence, and commitment—unwise. Conformity is the key to the crown—and, by extension, to success in our society."
—NEW YORK RADICAL WOMEN, "NO MORE MISS AMERICA" BROCHURE HANDED OUT IN ATLANTIC CITY, 1968

"Instruments of torture" such as girdles, bras, typewriters, makeup, and other symbols of femininity were tossed at the No More Miss America protest. Because organizers could not get a fire permit on the boardwalk, they were not burned.

THE GROUP New York Radical Women made their move against Miss America in September, setting up a series of demonstrations on the Atlantic City boardwalk and acting out their objections to the pageant's racism, militarism, contradictory messages about sexuality (the unbeatable Madonna-whore combination), consumerist spirit, and what they called its "encouragement of an American myth that oppresses men as well as women: the win-or-you're-worthless competitive disease."

Calling the pageant a cattle auction, they threw restrictive beauty products such as lash crimpers and girdles into a Freedom Trash Can and crowned a sheep with the Miss America tiara. Two members of the New Left, Tariq Ali and Susan Watkins, described the protest of 1968 in their historical work: "The protesters in Atlantic City gaily tossed away into a big dustbin all the symbols of women's docility and subservience that they could find."

Alongside their heated rhetoric the

New York Radical Women and allies protest at the Miss America pageant in Atlantic City, New Jersey.

protestors demonstrated a jocularity and spirit of fun that belied the later myth of the humorless feminist. Empowered by the drastic social changes happening across the nation, they took on the issue of women's objectification, something with which even the New Left radical movements struggled. In protesting Miss America they denounced not only beauty pageants but the values of the culture that produced them as degrading and insulting to all women. Until the Miss America protest, feminist issues had not received the kind of press coverage that more violent movements had commanded. The women's liberation movement protesters, however, took a more demanding approach, refusing to meet with male reporters and even breaking into the pageant during its live broadcast.

"At night, an 'inside squad' of twenty brave sisters disrupted the live telecast of the pageant itself, yodeling the eerie Berber yell (from *The Battle of Algiers*), shouting 'Freedom for Women!' and hanging a huge banner reading women's liberation from the balcony rail—all of which stopped the nationwide show for ten blood-curdling seconds." —ROBIN MORGAN, *GOING TOO FAR: THE PERSONAL CHRONICLE OF A FEMINIST*

OF COURSE, the Miss America protests were only the opening salvo for the women's liberation movement, which would prove adept at garnering media attention throughout the next decade, fundamentally changing much about expectations for middle-class white women in American society, even if their core public policy and equality agendas have remained unfulfilled. —M.N.

OCTOBER Power to the People

Tuesday 1
OCTOBER

Biologist and ecologist Stewart Brand publishes the first *Whole Earth Catalog*, which becomes an instant countercultural classic.

"A realm of intimate, personal power is developing—power of the individual to conduct his own education, find his own inspiration, shape his own environment, and share his adventure with whoever is interested." —STATEMENT OF PURPOSE, *WHOLE EARTH CATALOG*, 1968

Wednesday 2
OCTOBER

After a summer of protests against the Mexican government and the occupation of the central campus of the National Autonomous University (UNAM) by the army, a student demonstration in Mexico City ends with police, paratroopers, and paramilitary units firing on and killing scores of protesters.

Thursday 3
OCTOBER

American Independent Party presidential candidate George Wallace names noted hawk General Curtis LeMay as his running mate.

Thursday 10
OCTOBER

The Detroit Tigers defeat the St. Louis Cardinals, four games to three, to win baseball's World Series.

•

Barbarella, the erotic outer-space film starring Jane Fonda, hits the silver screen.

Wednesday 16
OCTOBER

Tommie "Jet" Smith and John Carlos, medalists in the 200-meter sprint at the Olympic Games in Mexico City, lower their heads and raise black-gloved fists during the playing of the national anthem, in protest of racism in the United States.

Sunday 20
OCTOBER

President John Kennedy's widow, Jacqueline Bouvier Kennedy, marries Greek shipping tycoon Aristotle Onassis.

Tuesday 22
OCTOBER

President Johnson signs into law the Gun Control Act of 1968. The act, along with the Safe Streets and Crime Control Act passed by Congress months earlier, contains the most significant restrictions on firearms since Congress enacted the National Firearms Act in 1934.

Friday 25
OCTOBER

Electric Ladyland, the third and final album by the Jimi Hendrix Experience, is released. The controversial original album cover depicting a group of nude women is soon replaced by a portrait of Hendrix singing.

Thursday 31
OCTOBER

President Johnson announces a complete halt to the bombing of North Vietnam in an attempt to restart stalled peace talks in Paris.

"What had more impact on me . . . was Black Power, in the sense of racial pride and self-esteem. It was a political statement to say, This is me. This is how I look. This is how I'm going to be. I am learning to accept myself and you'll have to accept me." —CAROLE MERRITT, ORAL HISTORY INTERVIEW

"The call for black power touched the depths of my soul . . . If we had had black power, my uncle would be alive; my grandfather, an unbent businessman; my father, a prosperous businessman and a city father in a predominantly black city; my mother, alive in cancer remission with the best of rehabilitation treatment; and me, never to have suffered the mental and emotional humiliation of being captive in a sanitarium. *Yes*, black power was the answer. The revolution to free black people was on the horizon . . . Black power demanded a strategy in which black people would transform the powerless black community into one that could exert its human potential to be an equal partner in the larger society."

—FORMER ACTIVIST GWEN PATTON, "BORN FREEDOM FIGHTER," 2010

BLACK POWER ROSE to prominence in the American consciousness in 1968, and October was the month that best encapsulated that shift.

Americans had already become all too familiar with the black leather jackets, black berets, and of course prominently displayed firearms that epitomized the Black Panther style. The Panthers' goals were also conveyed through public statements that sought to align the black freedom struggle in the United States with international Marxist revolution. In the end, though, these grandiose statements and embrace of violence interfered with the Panthers' abilities to achieve their goals of self-determination for black people, full employment, decent housing, and an end to police brutality, in part by alienating potential allies but also through exposing their own members and communities to increased surveillance and, ironically, police brutality.

Black Power became notorious for inflammatory rhetoric, but for many, including former Student Nonviolent Coordinating Committee activist Carole Merritt, once the voting rights bills were passed [in 1965], "there was nowhere to go" to address the de facto racism that endured: "The style of Black Power fit [these activists] very well, but it undermined the core of what made civil rights work for its day, which was nonviolence." SNCC itself, which once provided the "shock troops" of the civil rights movement, would prove unable to withstand the shift to violent protest and its 1969 name change to the Student National Coordinating Committee. After Stokely Carmichael and his successor H. Rap Brown left leadership positions in the SNCC to join the Black Panthers, the organization lost its effectiveness and ultimately collapsed.

NEVER A UNIFIED IDEOLOGY, Black Power took many forms, from the paramilitary posturing and community good works of the Black Panthers to natural hairstyles and African textiles and James Brown's "Say It Loud, I'm Black and I'm Proud," which sat at Number 1 on *Billboard*'s R&B chart all month.

FACING PAGE: Bookstores centered on African American and Third World history and culture, like Minneapolis, Minnesota's The Challenge, opened across the country. Here, manager Clarence S. Carter restocks his Afrocentric paperback collection.

"We wanted all the black people in the world—the little grocer, the man with the shoe repair store—to know that when that medal hangs on my chest or Tommie's, it hangs on his also." —JOHN CARLOS, INTERVIEW IN *LIFE*, NOVEMBER 1, 1968

ONE OF THE MOST visible Black Power gestures took place in October at the Summer Olympic Games in Mexico City. Tommie "Jet" Smith and John Carlos, medalists in the two-hundred-meter sprint, lowered their heads and raised black-gloved fists during the U.S. national anthem, in protest of racism in the United States. Though pictures of the event don't show it, Smith and Carlos accepted their medals barefoot, in recognition of the poverty that plagued black communities. Carlos had forgotten his gloves, so they each wore one of Smith's in a last-minute improvisation that quickly became symbolic of unity. The gesture led to them being stripped of their medals.

What Black Power movements and actions like this shared was an impulse to present the whole of black culture, however defined, to the broader culture; not just the parts that might reassure white allies but all that black people had been capable of despite discrimination and repression. The goal was to focus on collective, communal accomplishments rather than the breakthroughs of a chosen few.

Australian sprinter Peter Norman (silver) and Americans Tommie Smith (gold) and John Carlos (bronze) during the medal ceremony for the men's two-hundred-meter race.

CULTURAL NATIONALISM

Inspired by the passion and pride in Black Power actions and empowered by the legal equality the civil rights movement had won, members of other minority groups became politicized in vocal and visible ways. Radical representatives from a variety of ethnic groups rejected assimilation platforms in favor of cultural nationalism and liberation ideology. These groups, which included Latinos, Asian Americans, and Native Americans, were less prominent in white consciousness than African Americans had been. They attempted to change this by adopting many of the styles and techniques pioneered by organizations like the Black Panthers.

After comprehensive immigration reform passed in 1965, removing the ban on Asian immigration which had been in place, in one form or another, since 1882, increasing numbers of well-educated, professional families began to arrive in the United States from Asian nations and Latin America. Immigration more than doubled between 1965 and 1970, adding to the ranks of native-born African Americans, Latinos, and Asian Americans. As these groups grew, they expanded the critical analysis of the racial and economic politics of the United States beyond universities and into the communities most affected by injustice.

The leaders of the radical ethnic organizations were almost all young men, though this did not reflect their membership; many women were active participants. Yet much of the rhetoric of the movements, and particularly Black Power, focused on reclaiming the manhood many men felt they had lost or been denied by virtue of their skin color. Unfortunately, their manhood often manifested itself in the form of domination, particularly of women. As the movements grew and changed through the 1970s, black, Chicana, and Native feminist movements would emerge from women's critiques of the sexism in ethnic movements and the racism they encountered in second-wave feminism.

"It wasn't until later on in life that I realized that some of the things that happened to us as my brothers and sisters before me went to school, some of the things happened, it was because a lot of us had Spanish first names, and the teachers couldn't pronounce them, so they Anglicized our names or gave us a new name. You never read about us in the school books. Things on TV were the same thing; we weren't noticed on TV. If we were on TV we were the bandito, or we were the gardener. So there was little that reinforced that being a Mexican American was something to be proud of." —GILBERT DE LA O, CHICANO ACTIVIST, ORAL HISTORY INTERVIEW

WHILE NO ONE IS SURE of the etymology or exact meaning, "Chicano" and "Chicana" became the self-descriptors of choice for politicized Mexican Americans in 1968. The embrace of an amorphous Spanish-language term helped represent the activists' move away from Anglicized names and stereotypes and toward increased self-identification and community control.

The Chicano movement began in education. Protesting discrepancies in educational facilities, the exclusion of Mexican Americans and Mexican history from curriculums, and personal discrimination, organizers led walkouts in Los Angeles high schools and began to agitate for Chicano studies programs throughout the nation.

The Los Angeles walkouts ultimately involved over ten thousand students, which could not fail to draw attention. The protest was labeled "the birth of brown power" by the *Los Angeles Times,* and Robert F. Kennedy met with strikers during a visit to California in March.

Alongside the protests and rhetoric, many Mexican American and Puerto Rican youths were developing attitudes toward police, employment, and self-determination that were remarkably similar to those expressed by Black Power activists, even forming an organization focused on self-protection, called the Brown Berets. As Twin Cities Brown Beret member Gilbert de la O remembers, "You were protecting your community—you were there to serve, observe, and protect . . . As we got more organized, then we started talking about

Los Angeles Brown Berets adopted grassroots techniques to organize their communities.

education, we started talking about jobs, we started doing things in the community." The Brown Berets funded youth programs and opened a free clinic. Some of the developing organizations like the Brown Berets and the Young Lords (a Puerto Rican activist group) bore resemblances to street gangs but put their organizational efforts toward bettering their communities. These young men and women reminded Americans of their history—and future—as a multiracial society.

"The Brown Berets was the beginning of an identity, a beginning of us saying that we're here, we've been here all these years, we've been here all these generations, and we helped build America, we helped build Minnesota, and our rich history has either been neglected, distorted, or just ignored."
—GILBERT DE LA O, ORAL HISTORY INTERVIEW

LIKE ACTIVISTS in the Chicano and Black Power movements, the founders of the American Indian Movement were young urban men with legitimate grievances based in American history. AIM began when the largest urban Native American community in the country, located in Minneapolis, Minnesota, started to organize. AIM's demands for self-determination, employment, and housing were typical of many of the contemporary cultural nationalist organizations.

AIM's Indian Patrols were sent out to protect Native American communities from police brutality or at least to bear witness to hostile conditions and encounters. They brought the organization notoriety and success, and AIM expanded its goals and the scope of its operation, in particular focusing on ideas of sovereignty and reparations for the thousands of treaties the United States had made—and broken— with American Indian tribes.

AIM for Victory

Join hands at the American Indian Movement (AIM) National Convention, October 12,13,14 / Wild Rice Festival, October 15,16,17. For details, contact AIM, 1337 E. Franklin, Minneapolis, Minnesota 55408 (612) 333-4767

The American Indian Movement had roots in the counterculture and in urban Native American communities.

"The movement was founded to turn the attention of Indian people toward a renewal of spirituality which would impart the strength of resolve needed to reverse the ruinous policies of the United States, Canada, and other colonialist governments of Central and South America. At the heart of AIM is deep spirituality and a belief in the connectedness of all Indian people." —LAURA WATERMAN WITTSTOCK AND ELAINE J. SALINAS, "A BRIEF HISTORY OF THE AMERICAN INDIAN MOVEMENT," 2006

THE IDENTITY-BASED organizations also saw the importance of working together and, like the civil rights movement before them, creating alliances between communities with shared interests. Calling themselves the Third World Liberation Front, black, Asian American, Latino, and Native American students identified similar patterns of colonial repression and economic exploitation in their groups' histories in the United States. In November of 1968 they united to push for an ethnic studies department at San Francisco State University. Scholar Carlos Munoz Jr., one of the organizers of the Los Angeles walkouts, describes this as "the first time that Mexican American and other third world student activists united to create a politically explosive 'rainbow' coalition." The strike

"The Land Is Our Inheritance": cultural nationalist movements emphasized their connection to the land as part of their quest for self-determination.

ended in March 1969 when the university agreed to establish a school of ethnic studies, a victory for identity-based movements—and for the fuller understanding of the history and present of the United States as a multicultural nation. —E.A.

. . . .

MEXICO CITY, 1968

Like its neighbor to the north—indeed, like many societies across the globe in this year—Mexico was in the middle of a period of economic growth and stability in 1968. The International Olympic Committee selected Mexico to host the Summer Olympics (the first and only in Latin America until Rio de Janeiro 2016), and the country was eager to prove itself worthy of the honor. But young people were beginning to question the prosperity that had enabled them to continue their education. In *1968: The Year that Rocked the World,* Mark Kurlansky notes that Mexican students "were also aware that they had been the recipients of a growing economy that had not benefited many of the people around them"

and sought to take action that would better the lives of all Mexicans.

After student movements had taken off across Europe and the United States that spring, disrupting commerce and everyday life (to say the least), the Mexican government and the international community were concerned about the situation in Mexico, particularly as the date of the opening ceremony of the Olympic Games, scheduled for October 12, approached. Though President Diaz Ordaz and the Mexican government, as well as U.S. officials in Mexico, searched for evidence of foreign conspirators or an international ring of revolutionaries making their move in Mexico, the uprisings proved to be homegrown. The issues that inspired Mexican students in 1968 were mainly local: the protests of the late summer and early fall were sparked by police and military intervention in a fight between partisans of two local high schools, one of which was part of the National Autonomous University of Mexico (UNAM). After police arrested one hundred students who had occupied their school in protest, UNAM students spoke out and began to nonviolently organize against the repression and brutality, finding in it an issue that resonated with students and a wider Mexican public. The lack of violent inclinations shown by the protestors led the U.S. state department to label the protests "Embarrassing But Not a Threat to Stability."

By August 27, 1968, over one hundred thousand people gathered in the streets of Mexico City and its traditional gathering place, the Plaza del Zocalo. Student David Huerta remembered, "We didn't want to overthrow the government—we wanted some changes. It was really reasonable. It was nothing to be afraid of. After this huge demonstration, we felt sure that they could not say no to our demands." But they did; in his state of the union speech on September 1, President Diaz Ordaz flatly refused dialogue with the students, release of those who had been arrested in the course of demonstrating, or internal investigations into military and police brutality. His words had a chilling effect; by late September, activist Miguel Breseda remembered that "the movement was dwindling a little bit" and students were beginning to think that it might be time "to go back to school."

The rally the students held at Tlatelolco Plaza on October 2, only ten days before the Olympics were to begin, drew only "four to five thousand people. Nothing like the crowds in August," according to Huerta. The government had arranged soldiers and police all around the plaza; one faction began shooting, and after that all hell broke loose, with the police assuming the shots had come from the students and indiscriminately shooting at them in return. Rather than a peaceful press conference, the scene at Tlatelolco turned into a bloodbath as the police were able to block the only exit from the plaza, which was hemmed in by buildings on three sides. "The sound of automatic fire for two hours or more is one of the most consistent reports from witnesses," writes Kurlansky. Perhaps worse than the shooting was the silence that followed. Fear of repression ran so deep that families hesitated to ask after their missing children and friends didn't know if their comrades had survived or not; official death tolls ranged widely from an initial estimate of twelve up to forty, while unofficial numbers put the dead closer to 325. It's still not known exactly how many died at Tlatelolco.

The Olympic opening ceremonies proceeded without a hitch. —E.A.

Demonstrations in Mexico City on August 27 drew hundreds of thousands of students and supporters.

NOVEMBER The Votes Are In

Friday 1
NOVEMBER

The Motion Picture Association of America establishes the first film rating system, using the ratings of G for general audiences, M for mature audiences, R for restricted, and X for people 17 years or older.

"I knew that the mix of new social currents, the irresistible force of creators determined to make 'their' films (full of wild candor, groused some social critics), and the possible intrusion of government into the movie arena demanded my immediate action." —JACK VALENTI, MPAA PRESIDENT, "THE VOLUNTARY MOVIE RATINGS SYSTEM," 1991

Wednesday 6
NOVEMBER

Protesters begin a strike at San Francisco State University that will go on for five months. They demand equal access to public higher education, more senior faculty of color, and a new curriculum embracing the history and culture of ethnic minorities.

•

The trippy film *Head* starring the Monkees, the made-for-TV rock group, premieres in New York. One of the producers is little-known actor Jack Nicholson. *Head* flops at the box office, leading to the end for the "Pre-Fab Four."

Tuesday 5
NOVEMBER

Richard M. Nixon is elected president of the United States. He receives 43.4 percent of the popular vote to 42.7 percent for Democrat Hubert H. Humphrey, with independent candidate George Wallace making a strong showing at 13.5 percent.

•

Shirley Chisholm becomes the first African American woman elected to Congress, defeating Republican candidate James Farmer in the race for the U.S. House of Representatives seat from New York's Twelfth Congressional District.

Friday 22
NOVEMBER

The Beatles' self-titled double album, better known as *The White Album*, is released in the United States. It goes on to become their all-time best-selling album.

Saturday 23
NOVEMBER

At the annual football match between Harvard and Yale, the underdog Harvard team scores 16 points in the final 42 seconds to tie their archrivals, who were coming off a 16-game winning streak. The unlikely score inspires the *Harvard Crimson* to print the headline "Harvard Beats Yale, 29–29."

Sunday 24
NOVEMBER

Three Cuban men hijack Pan Am Flight 281 on a scheduled route to Puerto Rico and divert it to Havana—one of 15 Cuba-bound hijackings in 1968.

Tuesday 26
NOVEMBER

The rock supergroup Cream, featuring Eric Clapton, Ginger Baker, and Jack Bruce, play their farewell concert at London's Royal Albert Hall.

•

After gaining 3,187 yards and scoring 21 touchdowns for the University of Southern California during the 1968 season, running back O. J. Simpson wins the Heisman Trophy by the widest margin in Heisman history.

Nixon striking his signature double-V pose on the campaign trail in Philadelphia, Pennsylvania.

"As we look at America, we see cities enveloped in smoke and flame. We hear sirens in the night. We see Americans dying on distant battlefields abroad. We see Americans hating each other; fighting each other; killing each other at home. And as we see and hear these things, millions of Americans cry out in anguish. Did we come all this way for this? Listen to the answer . . . It is the quiet voice in the tumult and the shouting. It is the voice of the great majority of Americans, the forgotten Americans." —RICHARD M. NIXON, NOMINATION ACCEPTANCE SPEECH, REPUBLICAN NATIONAL CONVENTION, AUGUST 8, 1968

THE 1968 PRESIDENTIAL ELECTION is considered one of the most significant in history. Nixon's win for the Republicans prompted a major political realignment. From 1933 to 1968, Democrats—riding the wave of the New Deal liberal politics defined by President Franklin Roosevelt—won seven out of nine presidential elections. But from 1968 to 2008, Republicans won seven out of ten presidential elections.

In 1968 the Democratic consensus quickly broke apart over debates about civil rights, law-and-order issues, "permissiveness," and the conduct of the Vietnam War. White Southerners, once reliably Democratic, shifted decisively to Republican ranks. Hubert H. Humphrey—a Northern New Deal Democrat— won less than 10 percent of the white Southern vote. From 1968 to 2008 only two Democrats,

Jimmy Carter and Bill Clinton, were elected president, and both were native Southerners. Not until 2008 was a Northern Democrat, Barack Obama, again elected president.

THE CANDIDATES OF 1968

Lyndon B. Johnson [Democratic Party]

Lyndon B. Johnson (1908–73) ascended to the presidency after the assassination of John F. Kennedy in 1963. One year later he ran for the office and was elected by the largest electoral margin up to that time. Johnson and his Great Society programs enjoyed tremendous popular support, but by 1967 his presidency was crippled by America's involvement in the

Vietnam War. On March 31, 1968, at the end of a televised speech about the war, Johnson announced that he would not seek or accept his party's nomination for another term as president.

Eugene McCarthy [Democratic Party]

Eugene McCarthy (1916–2005) was a U.S. senator from Minnesota who, in November 1967, announced his candidacy for the Democratic nomination—a direct challenge to President Johnson. McCarthy's strong and principled stance against the Vietnam War attracted hundreds of thousands of young supporters and volunteers. The campaign sputtered, however, and McCarthy's momentum was halted in March 1968 by the entry into the race of Senator Robert F. Kennedy.

Robert F. Kennedy [Democratic Party]

Robert F. Kennedy (1925–68) had served as attorney general in the administration of his brother, John F. Kennedy, and continued in that office under President Johnson. A liberal champion of civil and economic rights, Kennedy was elected to the U.S. Senate from New York in 1964 and soon broke with President Johnson over the issue of the war. He jumped into the race for the Democratic nomination in March, just days after the New Hampshire primary, where McCarthy had come close to defeating the president. On June 5, just moments after declaring victory in the California primary, Kennedy was shot and mortally wounded by Sirhan Sirhan, a Palestinian American.

Johnson and Nixon had a long history together. Here they are meeting at the White House before Nixon assumed the presidency.

George S. McGovern [Democratic Party]

George S. McGovern (born 1922) was representing his home state of South Dakota in the U.S. Senate in 1968 when he found himself "drafted" as a successor candidate to the slain Robert Kennedy. McGovern had distinguished himself in the Senate as an early and vigorous opponent of the Vietnam War. He announced his candidacy just two weeks before the nominating convention, where he would eventually receive fewer than 150 delegate votes, far behind Humphrey and McCarthy. Senator McGovern did become the party's nominee in 1972, losing the election to the incumbent president, Richard Nixon.

Hubert H. Humphrey [Democratic Party]

Hubert H. Humphrey (1911–78), a former senator from Minnesota, was elected vice president in 1964 under President Johnson. In August 1968 he became the Democratic Party nominee for president at the rancorous Chicago convention. A classic New Deal liberal, Humphrey struggled in the campaign to become his own man, independent of the twinned curse of the unpopular Johnson and the disaster of Vietnam. In the run-up to the election Humphrey was far behind his Republican opponent but pulled very close in the waning days of October, only to lose narrowly to Nixon on November 5.

Richard M. Nixon [Republican Party]

Richard M. Nixon (1913–94) had served as vice president for eight years under President Eisenhower but lost his own bid for president to John F. Kennedy in 1960. Two years later he ran for governor of California and lost. But in 1968 Nixon ran a modern, effective campaign for the Republican nomination, becoming virtually unstoppable at the Miami convention. In the general election Nixon won over many potential Wallace voters by appealing to the racist fears of Southern whites. He narrowly edged out his Democratic rival, Hubert H. Humphrey, in the popular vote but won a resounding majority in the Electoral College.

Humphrey's campaign materials ranged from the ridiculous to the sublime.

Nelson Rockefeller [Republican Party]

Nelson Rockefeller (1908−79), who had served as New York governor since 1959, formally entered the race for the 1968 Republican presidential nomination shortly before the start of the convention, held in Miami in early August. A liberal Republican, Rockefeller polled third on the convention's first ballot, behind both the conservative Ronald Reagan and the more moderate Richard Nixon, the eventual nominee. In 1974 Rockefeller was appointed vice president by President Gerald R. Ford, who had succeeded to the office after President Nixon's resignation.

Ronald W. Reagan [Republican Party]

Former Hollywood star Ronald W. Reagan (1911−2004) came to national political prominence with his ringing endorsement of presidential nominee Barry Goldwater at the 1964 Republican National Convention. A staunch anti-Communist conservative espousing a return to law and order, Reagan was elected governor of California in 1966. He already had presidential ambitions, however, and was soon making moves toward the 1968 nomination. At the Miami convention in August 1968 he came in a distant second to Richard Nixon. Ronald Reagan was the party's nominee in 1980; after defeating incumbent president Jimmy Carter, he served two terms as president, from 1981 to 1989.

George C. Wallace [American Independent Party]

Former governor of Alabama George C. Wallace (1919−98) ran for president in 1968 on the American Independent Party ticket. A colorful populist and avowed segregationist, Wallace had been making headlines since the early 1960s with his opposition to school integration. Wallace eventually won enough votes in November to carry five states, all in the Deep South. Wallace sought the presidency in three subsequent elections.

Eldridge Cleaver [Peace and Freedom Party]

In the fifties and sixties, Eldridge Cleaver (1935−98) served time in prison for rape and assault. Released in 1966, he joined the radical Black Panther Party, becoming its minister of information. In 1968 he published *Soul on Ice,* a book of essays about black America written while he was in prison, and the same year mounted a largely symbolic campaign for president, running on the Peace and Freedom Party platform. Cleaver was on the ballot in just twelve states and, because he was only thirty-three, would have been ineligible to be president had he been elected.

NIXON'S THE ONE

Richard M. Nixon served as vice president for eight years under Dwight D. Eisenhower (1953−61) but lost his own bid for president to John F. Kennedy in 1960. Two years later he ran for governor of California and

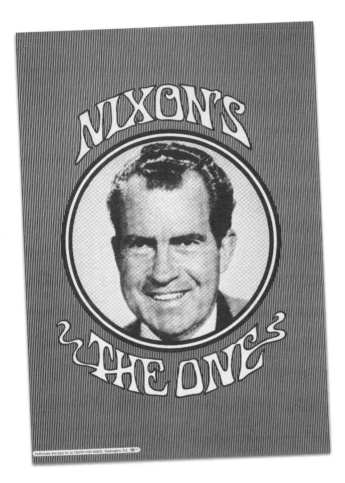

LEFT: Even Nixon's campaign tried to hop aboard the psychedelic bandwagon. ABOVE: Young Nixon supporters in Atlanta, Georgia.

lost, bitterly telling reporters at what he said would be his last press conference that they wouldn't "have Nixon to kick around anymore." In 1962, in both popular opinion and by his own admission, Nixon's political career seemed to be over. And so it was for a while. He read the political tea leaves and avoided the 1964 presidential race, leaving it to conservative standard-bearer Barry Goldwater to take the Republican Party down in flames as he lost to President Johnson. By 1966 Nixon was edging back into the spotlight, and by the following year, it was clear to all observers that he was running for president—again. As 1968 opened Nixon was fully expected to win the nomination and, in November, to defeat the increasingly unpopular incumbent, Lyndon B. Johnson.

Still, a cloud of suspicion and anxiety hung over Nixon and filled the airwaves and the media as the positioning and the campaigning ramped up. Early in March 1968, *Look* magazine ran an article called "The Puzzling Case of Richard Nixon" by novelist Fletcher Knebel (coauthor of 1962's best-selling *Seven Days in May*). The piece is illustrated by a flattering Norman Rockwell portrait, but there's also an almost comically malevolent photo of a shifty-eyed Dick Nixon, too. The article concludes: "And so, candidate Nixon of 1968: Hawk abroad, flexible innovator at home, a loser on the comeback trail, the old pro in the familiar, dusty road of a national campaign, a man who has learned to exploit the likelihood that he'll never win a beauty prize, the loner, the hustler, the riddle."

Nixon himself had no such doubts. Carefully amassing primary victories and convention delegates, Nixon ran a brilliant campaign for the Republican nomination, holding to the middle and fending off challenges from moderate Nelson Rockefeller and conservative Ronald Reagan. At the relatively uneventful Republican convention in Miami, Nixon coasted to an easy first-ballot win and selected Maryland governor Spiro T. Agnew as his running mate.

In the general election campaign, Nixon adopted a "Southern strategy" by appealing to the racist fears of Southern whites, winning over many who may have otherwise cast their votes for segregationist and third-party candidate George Wallace. Nixon ran on a strong law-and-order platform, blaming Democrats—especially President Johnson and, by association, Vice President Humphrey, who became Nixon's Democratic opponent at the end of August—for the nation's slide into "permissiveness" and racial unrest. Nixon also promised to bring a successful end to the Vietnam War and to end the draft.

On November 5 the American electorate, battle-weary from the violence of 1968, went to the polls. But the numbers were so close that everyone went to bed on election night without a concession from the loser or a victory speech from the winner. In the end, Republican Richard Nixon prevailed over Humphrey by just 512,000 votes—about one percent of the total popular vote. George Wallace garnered enough votes in five Southern states to win them outright—the last third-party presidential candidate to carry any states in the Electoral College. On the Congressional side things didn't look so good for the new president: Nixon entered the White House as the first president in more than a century to start off without a majority of his own party in both houses of Congress.

In a postmortem on the election, *Life* magazine reminded readers that the campaign had been marked by "rousing unenthusiasm" for the candidates and that "the overworked word *charisma* dropped from the political vocabulary, because there was no one to apply it to." But *Life* thought that Nixon was the better of the two major candidates and hoped that, even in a "year of such shock and cleavage," the new president would do as he had promised: bring us together. —B.H.

ABOVE: This button may have seemed ironic to some, but others believed Nixon could win the war.

. . . .

ONE DISCORDANT NOTE AFTER ANOTHER

The two leading pop-cultural barometers of the era mostly sat out the marquee events of 1968. Bob Dylan, still recovering from a motorcycle accident, returned early in the year with the release of the oddly quiet, elliptical, and understated *John Wesley Harding*, a tentative step backward from his 1966 masterpiece *Blonde on Blonde*.

Dylan's earlier songs and records, though, were still in heavy rotation in dorm rooms, crash pads, and gathering places all over the country, and "The Times They Are A-Changing," "Blowing in the Wind," "Masters of War," and "Subterranean Homesick Blues" remained anthems of the far-flung movements of 1968.

Dylan himself, however, was strangely absent—and silent—throughout the year's escalating demonstrations, marches, protests, and riots, and his subsequent records would increasingly eschew anything resembling grand political pronouncements.

Billboard magazine's 1968 artist of the year Jimi Hendrix, did have a Top 10 single with a blistering version of Dylan's "All Along the Watchtower" (from *John Wesley Harding*), and many other artists—including Joan Baez—recorded Dylan's songs that year.

As they had already done so many other times, the Beatles tapped into the counterculture early—the two preceding years had seen the release of *Sgt. Pepper's Lonely Hearts Club Band* and *Magical Mystery Tour*, both indelible and typically emblematic of their time and place—but by 1968 the group seemed burned-out and disengaged from a scene they'd been instrumental in helping to create. Even so, 1968 was a weird and busy year for the band,

but in ways that were strangely at odds with what was happening in the United States and around the world.

Early in the year, John and George traveled to India for transcendental meditation studies with the Maharishi Mahesh Yogi, and they were eventually joined by Paul and Ringo. Following that trip—and once again they were ahead of the curve—the rest of 1968 seemed like one discordant note after another. The Beatles created their own label, Apple, complete with posh new headquarters at 3 Seville Road, as well as an ill-fated boutique (which did not survive the year). They began recordings for what became known as *The White Album*. John and Paul made an appearance on *The Tonight Show with Johnny Carson*, but in one of the more absurd cultural juxtapositions of that or any year, the folksy former baseball player Joe Garagiola was the guest host the night of their appearance, and the experience was so awkward that John later called it "the most embarrassing thing I've ever been on."

June Asher broke off her engagement with McCartney and Cynthia Lennon filed for divorce from John. Ringo walked out of a session for *The White Album* and, as a result, Paul provided the drum track on "Back in the U.S.S.R." There was some good news: the August 26 release of "Hey Jude / Revolution" sold wildly and eventually became the band's biggest-selling single.

There were more television appearances (*David Frost, The Smothers Brothers*). *The White Album* was completed. John had taken up with Yoko Ono, and the couple was arrested on drug charges after their apartment was raided. Then, late in the year, there was a flurry of activity that served as a sort of time-lapse state-of-the-disunion snapshot of both the disintegration of the band and the general weirdness of the times.

For a couple weeks in November the Beatles were engaged in a furious and disorienting bit of pop-cultural fast-forward and rewind: on November 11, Apple released the *Unfinished Music No. 1: Two Virgins* LP by John and Yoko; two days later the film version of *Yellow Submarine* appeared in U.S. theaters. Finally, in the last week of the month, *The White Album* went on sale, debuting at number one on both the U.S. and U.K. charts, and Lennon was convicted for possession of marijuana.

In hindsight, the fragmented, chaotic, frequently abrasive, and often deliberately incoherent *White Album* seems like a dissolute product from a much later year, but listening to it today it sounds like a perfect, exhausted distillation of the static and discord of 1968, a sprawling, messy summation of not just the year but of the years immediately preceding and following.

Contrast "Revolution's" mix of skepticism, disengagement, and *almost* hopeful resignation ("We all want to change the world / But when you talk about destruction / Don't you know that you can count me out / Don't you know it's going to be all right") with the Rolling Stones' "Street Fighting Man" (also released in 1968) or any other of the iconic songs of that year, and it's hard not to conclude that—a year before Woodstock and the Manson murders, and four years before Watergate and the last gasps of the Vietnam War—the Beatles saw the end coming long before anyone else.

Fittingly, perhaps, the Fab Four closed out the year with their annual fan club Christmas record, which featured Tiny Tim performing a ukulele version of "November Man," poems by John, and a warped sample of "Helter Skelter."

It somehow seems apt that by the close of 1968, both the Beatles and Bob Dylan, having provided so much of the fuel for the countercultural zeitgeist, had essentially abdicated their roles as any kind of spokesmen for their generation. —B.Z.

Interlude
FASHION, DESIGN, CONSUMERISM

"No one can win against kipple . . . It's a universal principle: the entire universe is moving toward a final state of total, absolute kippleization."

—PHILIP K. DICK, *DO ANDROIDS DREAM OF ELECTRIC SHEEP?*

PHILIP K. DICK'S 1968 science-fiction classic *Do Androids Dream of Electric Sheep?* is considered one of his best novels (and was the basis for the 1982 film *Blade Runner*). Set on an Earth devastated by nuclear weapons and fallout, the book's world retains advanced city technologies and infrastructures, and in many ways reflects the 1960s' riotous growth in consumerism. Dick coined the word "kipple" to refer to the accumulation of useless objects in people's lives. People in the 1960s developed a variety of strategies to deal with this accumulation.

In April 1968 *Reader's Digest* published an article called "How Can You Lose a Swimming Pool," condensed from a somewhat longer piece in the *Denver Post* Sunday magazine. *Reader's Digest* cast a fairly wide net for its articles, gathering them not just from national magazines but also from the American heartland. This allowed *Digest* editors to keep their finger on the pulse of America, especially for lifestyle articles. At first glance satirical and

lighthearted (the *Digest* was well known for leavening each issue with wholesome humor), the article sounded themes that were beginning to be heard in 1968, a violent and divisive year, yes, but also a year that was the high-water mark of the postwar age of affluence. Consumer goods proliferated after the war,

Midcentury modern style met bright colors to encourage people to buy the newest of everything, including modular dishware, in 1968.

138

and the pace of production and consumption just kept accelerating in the turbulent 1960s, especially in suburbia.

Prosperity brought with it new pressures and new anxieties about class and status. The tidal waves of consumer goods also produced a new problem, described by "How Can You Lose a Swimming Pool" author Will Stanton:

> "I happen to be a member of the new affluent middle class. My neighbors are in the same bracket and we all have the same problem—one unique to our country and time. There's no place to put anything . . . There's no limit to what money can buy—and that's the root of the problem . . . There used to be rich people and poor people. The poor had no room to keep things in, but they didn't have anything to keep anyhow. The people that owned all the stuff had castles. It worked out fine."

When Stanton and his wife, Ethel, bought their house, he writes, "the thing that impressed us was the size . . . We had always lived in an apartment. Then suddenly we had all that space and all the beautiful catalogues and charge accounts everywhere." They also had two kids, then three (that's when they bought a station wagon and then a second car); they developed hobbies (restoring furniture, photography, gardening), all of which consumed space and demanded more consumption; they bought a boat, "because the children would only be young once," but they had to keep it in their ever-shrinking yard. They bought a large, portable pool that some-

how got lost one year when it was packed away amidst all the rest of the stuff. Will didn't want to tell anybody, because he was worried that people wouldn't understand: "The trouble is some people are 50 years beyond the times. They just don't understand the problems of the affluent middle class."

One solution was the creation of the U.S. self-storage industry (U-Store-It, Stor-More, et al.), which began in the mid-1960s and expanded rapidly in the following decade. By 2011, rentable self-storage units in the United States accounted for more than 2.35 billion square feet of storage.

The batik tunic was a hallmark of hippie dress, as was the irreverent Ringo for President button.

IN 1968, MAGAZINES like *Reader's Digest* and the *Saturday Evening Post* were fond of trend pieces based on this formula: "Look at what those kids are (fill in the blank) now!" The blank could be filled in any number of ways: "wearing," "saying," "listening to," "smoking," "drinking," "watching." Magazine editors and photographers loved the counterculture (or at least their own image of it). "Those kids" made great pictures, they made great copy, and they sold magazines. And if you could layer onto this head-shaking voyeurism a veneer of scholarly perspicacity, all the better.

"The mini-skirt, of course, is not a fashion. It is a return to the tribal costume worn by men and women alike in all oral societies. As our world moves from hardware to software, the mini-skirt is a major effort to reprogram our sensory lives in a tribal pattern of tactility and involvement." —MARSHALL MCLUHAN, QUOTED IN "THE BIG COSTUME PUT-ON," *SATURDAY EVENING POST*, JULY 27, 1968

AN ONLY SLIGHTLY less-sophisticated take on the year's fashion was provided by Bill Emerson, the *Post*'s editor. In "The Big Costume Put-On," subtitled "What They're Wearing Instead of Clothes," Emerson defined his terms: "'They' is not us, the middle-class more than a little conservative grown-ups who read the *Post*. 'They' is, simply put, American youth." As Emerson explains, "The turned-on people of today wear all sorts of extraordinary things instead of clothes . . . It looks as if that curious subculture known as youth has ambushed us fogy-boppers with their costumes and is firing away. The ammunition is not deadly, but it does make you feel angry and 150 years old."

Buttressed by a photo essay deeper in the magazine featuring numerous young people bedecked in slightly Edwardian or Indian or Elizabethan or military surplus or even

Broad collars and fringed vests were also considered quite fashionable, but only if paired with shaggy facial hair.

vintage American fashions, Emerson waxes anthropological: "Man is changing his attitude about himself . . . This mind-boggling costume party has a much more serious message than simple disguise. It may well be a part of a ritual effort to isolate a personality, and there is some question as to what will emerge."

Another magazine popular in 1968 was *EYE,* a short-lived effort by the Hearst Corporation to cash in on the exploding youth market (and, of course, in advertising profits). Hearst was already publishing *Cosmopolitan, Good Housekeeping, House Beautiful,* and

Harper's Bazaar. EYE, judging by its advertisements for makeup, perfumes, hair products, more makeup, handbags, and Wonder Bread ("Don't forget this: Boys love to eat. And they love Wonder sandwiches.") was largely meant for younger female readers and didn't seem to offer them values significantly outside the mainstream created by other Hearst publications.

More serious people might have been reading *Evergreen* that year. One of America's leading literary magazines, heavily laced with helpings of leftist politics, *Evergreen*'s February issue reproduced speeches and letters by Fidel Castro and by Cuban revolutionary Che Guevara, captured and killed just a few months earlier. The winter 1968 issue, featuring Paul Davis's stunning portrait of Guevara on the cover, marked the beginning of the secular canonization of Che. In fact, this was the first time this iconic image (based on a 1960 photograph) was published in the United States.

Evergreen was not a cheap, flaming radical rag; its newsstand price of one dollar was significantly higher than weeklies like *Life* (thirty cents an issue) or the *New Yorker* (which jumped to fifty cents an issue in Septem-

ber). There are ads inside: mostly for records (Judy Collins, Arlo Guthrie, Janis Ian); book clubs and publishers (including some offering "homosexual theme fiction"); and a great two-page ad for art posters, the source of the Picasso "Don Quixote" prints that hung on untold thousands of college dorm room walls.

Evergreen seems, in retrospect, to be an almost uncannily precise evocation of that pervasive phenomenon of the 1960s trenchantly described two years later by Tom Wolfe as "radical chic." Radical chic kept some of the political elements of leftist struggle, but it focused heavily on an aura of danger and outsiderism, while "hip consumerism," like that of *EYE,* sought to disconnect the signature visual and aural elements of hipness and the counterculture from any subversive or political meanings they might have been associated with. Just as easily, paisley, macramé, Eastern mysticism, and Che Guevara could be converted into commodities. The counterculture could be an effective bandwagon for making money, even for corporations as historically identified with the conservative Establishment as Hearst.

ABOVE: Everything, from sunglasses to bag to scarf, was an opportunity to demonstrate taste and style. RIGHT: Even vegetables received the "groovy" treatment.

DECEMBER In the Beginning

Tuesday 3
DECEMBER

Following a long decline in both his music and acting careers, Elvis Presley's '68 Comeback Special airs on NBC, marking the return of the "King of Rock 'n' Roll."

Monday 9
DECEMBER

Douglas Engelbart and fellow researchers unveil their "writing machine" at Stanford University. The world's first word processor features the first "mouse" and the ability to call up documents, cut and paste text, create hyperlinks, and communicate with others over a network.

Friday 20
DECEMBER

Two high school students are shot to death while parked on a lovers' lane in Benicia, California—the first victims of a serial murderer who comes to be known as the Zodiac Killer.

Wednesday 11
DECEMBER

The Rolling Stones Rock and Roll Circus—a special event featuring performances by the Stones, the Who, Taj Mahal, Jethro Tull, and John Lennon and Yoko Ono—is filmed on a soundstage in London. The film is not released until 1996.

Sunday 22
DECEMBER

Julie Nixon, daughter of president-elect Richard Nixon, marries David Eisenhower, grandson of former president Dwight D. Eisenhower, in New York.

•

An eight-day truce is declared in the year-long war between Nigeria and the secessionist state of Biafra, a brutal conflict that led to shocking massacres and widespread starvation.

Monday 23
DECEMBER

Nearly a year after the capture of the USS *Pueblo* by North Korean forces, representatives of the United States and North Korea meet at Panmunjom, Korea, and sign an agreement for the crew's release.

Tuesday 24
DECEMBER

On a worldwide television broadcast, the crew of *Apollo 8*, orbiting the moon, send back the first images of Earthrise and read from the book of Genesis.

Thursday 26
DECEMBER

Psychedelic drug proponent and counterculture leader Dr. Timothy Leary is arrested in Laguna Beach, California, for possession of a small amount of marijuana, which Leary claims was planted by the arresting officer. He is later convicted.

"If you are serious about your religion, if you really wish to commit yourself to the spiritual quest, you must learn how to use psychochemicals. Drugs are the religion of the twenty-first century. Pursuing the religious life today without using psychedelic drugs is like studying astronomy with the naked eye because that's how they did it in the first century A.D., and besides telescopes are unnatural"

—TIMOTHY LEARY, *THE POLITICS OF ECSTASY*

Tuesday 31
DECEMBER

By the year's end the number of U.S. troops in Vietnam has reached the all-time peak of 549,000. The U.S. death toll for 1968 is the highest yearly total in the war's history—nearly 17,000 soldiers killed in action.

"In the closing days of 1968, all mankind could exult in the vision of a new universe. For all its upheavals and frustrations, the year would be . . . celebrated as the year in which men saw at first hand their little earth entire, a remote, blue-brown sphere hovering like a migrant bird in the hostile night of space." —*TIME*, JANUARY 3, 1969, NAMING THE *APOLLO 8* ASTRONAUTS THE 1968 MEN OF THE YEAR

IN RETROSPECTIVES of the 1960s, particularly of 1968—so dominated by violence, war, and racial conflict, by sex, drugs, and rock and roll—it is easy to forget that the decade was also intensely focused on scientific and technological breakthroughs. Science was making tremendous advances in the 1960s, due in large part to increased government monies to universities and research institutions. Popular interest in scientific thought and achievements was also reaching new heights.

Popular Science magazine, which for years had featured cover stories on wildly futuristic inventions, had by the 1960s shifted its attention to what might best be understood as a conflation of science and consumerism, reflecting the era's relative prosperity. The February 1968 issue, for example, analyzed (in a very scientific way, of course) the top ten color TVs. Other cover stories that year included "Tires for Your Car" and "Your TV Antenna May Be Out of Date!"

Science fiction in 1968 offered variations on recognizably sixties themes. Philip K. Dick's landmark 1968 novel *Do Androids Dream of Electric Sheep?* foresaw a future (way

Apollo 8 blasting off at the Kennedy Space Center, Merritt Island, Florida.

out in 1992) in which people—actual humans, not the near-perfect "replicants" created by science—can dial up any mood or feeling with drugs and machines. One of the 1968 nominees for the Hugo for best science-fiction novel was *The Butterfly Kid,* set in a future where drugs are used to change reality. And there were any number of science-fact articles in popular magazines that described credible futures along similar lines.

In "Pyschochemistry: Personality by Prescription" (*Playboy,* November 1968), Ernest Havemann, a journalist and psychologist, writes, "Man will soon have drugs that will cure his major mental disturbances, eliminate his fears and anxieties, keep him fat or lean at will, let him decide for himself how long, if at all, he cares to sleep, make him much smarter than ever before, and even permit him to live longer. You name it, and there is somebody—not a wild-eyed visionary but a sane and skeptical scientist—who believes it is just around the corner."

On the nonfiction best-seller lists in 1968, jostling for rank with diet books and cookbooks, were several strikingly influential books on science. James Watson's *The Double Helix,* described as "a personal account of the discovery of the structure of DNA," was something of a publishing sensation that spring and summer, selling well on college campuses but also to adults eager to learn something about DNA, that mysterious acronym that had been cropping up in conversations and that contained, perhaps, some clue to the meaning of life. Desmond Morris's *The Naked Ape* also sold exceptionally well that year. A breezy stroll through the science of human evolution and biology, with cover art (on some editions) of the backsides of naked people and an explanation of the evolution of breasts and genitalia, it was a book that could make science almost sexy.

Paul Ehrlich's *The Population Bomb* was more polemic than academically rigorous science but contained an alarming wake-up call about overpopulation and the collapse of human systems worldwide. Ehrlich's work, like Garrett Hardin's widely disseminated article "The Tragedy of the Commons" (first published in the journal *Science* in 1968), became a foundational document for the environmental movement that emerged in the 1970s.

But more than anything else, "science" in the public eye in 1968 was identified with breathtaking advances in two fields: medicine and space exploration.

A new day in medicine had dawned at the end of 1967 with the first human-to-human heart transplants in history, performed in South Africa by Dr. Christiaan Barnard, who became an international celebrity. In a matter of weeks there was a virtual "space race" in risky heart operations, with doctors on several continents one-upping each other.

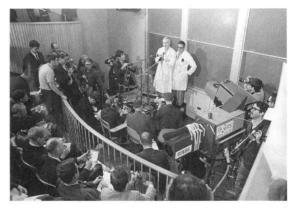

Drs. Norman Shumway (left) and Donald Harrison announce the first successful heart transplant in the United States, at Stanford University in California. A fifty-four-year-old steelworker received the heart of a forty-five-year-old man and survived for fourteen days after the operation.

The first successful adult heart transplants in the United States—with patient survival measured in months instead of days—came in 1968. The pace of transplantation, and the heightening of public interest in it, intensified during the period from 1968 to 1970, before slowing due to poor outcomes and an increase in other approaches to treating heart disease. Another transplant therapy launched in 1968, however, grew rapidly in the coming decades: bone-marrow transplantation. First performed at the University of Minnesota hospitals, bone-marrow transplants are now a standard and highly successful therapy for adults and children with leukemia, lymphoma, and many other conditions.

Even more than the stunning advances in medicine, the year in science was dominated by visions—real and cinematic—of space exploration. Stanley Kubrick's "mind-blowing" epic *2001: A Space Odyssey* opened in April 1968 and became not only one of the year's biggest box-office hits but also a critical paradigm for popular understanding of the future in space. The film was memorable for its visuals, with hypnotically gliding spaceships and zero-gravity interiors. Even more penetrating was the character of HAL, the machine with a suave voice and a menacing soul, who became the embodiment—or rather, the opposite of embodiment—of fears and expectations about artificial intelligence and science run amok.

This popular culture apogee of space exploration was set against a real-life backdrop provided by none other than the U.S. government: the spectacular successes of NASA's

The research team at SRI demonstrated computing technologies that would not be widely available for decades.

space program. Gone were Cold War worries about Soviets outpacing Americans. In 1968 alone, the Apollo program launched no fewer than four missions—two of them manned—in pursuit of the goal of landing men on the moon. *Apollo 8,* carrying three astronauts, was launched just before Christmas and provided the waning days of 1968—this year of shock and violence, horror and despair—with an indelibly uplifting note. On Christmas Eve, Jim Lovell, William Anders, and Frank Borman became the first humans to orbit the moon. They saw the Earthrise and sent televised images of the moon's surface back to Earth, reading from the book of Genesis: "In the beginning . . ." —B.H.

NASA presented this model of *Apollo 8* to Vice President Hubert Humphrey.

"A hundred lunar distances in space are really nothing. You haven't gone anywhere—not even to the next planet. So here was this orb looking like a Christmas tree ornament, very fragile, not an infinite expanse of granite, and seemingly of a physical insignificance, and yet it was our home." —WILLIAM ANDERS, *APOLLO 8* LUNAR MODULE PILOT, JOHNSON SPACE CENTER ORAL HISTORY PROJECT, 1997

Earthrise, taken by astronaut William Anders aboard *Apollo 8,* was one of the most iconic images of the year, gracing the cover of *Life* and countless other magazines then and since.

EPILOGUE

Brad Zellar

I'M PRETTY SURE that I can trace my first raw and fully formed constellation of memories to 1968. I turned seven that year and recognized, maybe for the first time, the sources of tension in the adults in my life. The world outside my own became a part of my memories that year, and time and again I saw the extent to which that bigger outside world affected *my* world—and the people around me.

I'm talking about powerful, visceral, permanent memories, a string of interrelated mental images that even then were changing the world I lived in, a world that I was beginning to understand was big, complex, weird, violent, and potentially marvelous and ripe with all sorts of explosive opportunities.

The things that were happening—and there were all sorts of things happening, all over the world—were on the television, of course, but also in the daily newspapers and in the magazines I used to look at on my frequent visits with my mother, siblings, and friends to the public library downtown, a place that was the one reliable refuge of my childhood and the sole place that didn't seem to have any interest in keeping secrets from children.

I remember the palpable anxiousness and tension of the adults in my world. They were asking questions of each other and

shaking their heads a lot, and the conversations around barbecue grills and out and about in town had an unfamiliar gravity. They didn't know what was happening, obviously; couldn't understand. A kid understands when the adults don't understand, and that always tends to make things more interesting.

I have a memory of sitting on the floor with my mother as she silently folded laundry and we watched the breaking news of Robert Kennedy's assassination in Los Angeles.

I also remember watching reports from Vietnam and being puzzled and spooked in a way that I had never felt before. The period footage from that war was so raw and murky and full of terrifying noise. It apparently hadn't yet occurred to the networks to attempt to heighten the dramatic gravity of such dispatches by pairing the footage with Barber's "Adagio for Strings."

Ours was a small town of almost entirely white faces, located smack-dab in the middle of the middle of the country, but because it was a small town with a slaughterhouse, the war brought everything that was happening back to us in one way or another. Local boys who were otherwise destined to follow their fathers into the meat-packing plant were drafted or joined the military to postpone the inevitable. They went off to war and some of them came home in coffins. Hippies and antiwar protestors made appearances in the Fourth of July parade. (The counterculture, however tentatively embraced by a small group of young people in town, stood out in even sharper relief as a result.)

It was a predominantly blue-collar town, and I remember that something like *Laugh-In* didn't make a whole lot of sense at the time. We just regarded it as a bit of daffy exotica, which it essentially was. Even Rowan and Martin in their tuxedos looked like two squares presiding over something they didn't quite understand.

The whole time would have been dizzying enough even without the rockets—spaceships, finally!—but the rockets took things to a whole other level of wondrous surrealism. We saw astronauts in their brilliant and vaguely terrifying suits. We saw Earth from space for the first time. On trips to the Piggly Wiggly we begged our mother to buy Tang. On Halloween we dressed as hippies and GI Joes and trick-or-treated side by side. It was as if the world had suddenly turned into a two-way funhouse mirror.

There were contradictions everywhere you looked, but the nation as a whole was no better equipped to see contradictions in 1968 than it is today.

Politics in a small town are always complex, but that was a year that sorely tested all sorts of friendships and family ties. And the politics of 1968 didn't exactly make much sense. George Wallace, the segregationist

Checking yarn for making ribbon at a 3M factory in Fairmont, Minnesota.

governor of Alabama who ran for president, was a Democrat—an old-school Southern Democrat, but still. He won five states. And despite a year of growing and increasingly violent protests against the war (1968 was by far the high-water mark for U.S. casualties in Vietnam), and despite the fact that the voting age was still twenty-one and boys as young as seventeen were dying in the conflict and the draft was escalating by the month, both major parties nominated hawks at their conventions.

Despite a time of virtually unprecedented comfort and a booming middle class, the country was still facing tremendous economic disparity, particularly among blacks in the inner cities and the South.

The struggle for peace was often violent. More cognitive dissonance. And as large as the civil rights, antiwar, and countercultural movements loom in the events of the year, ultimately none of them could produce a charismatic figure with any serious mainstream influence to replace the slain Martin Luther King Jr. and Robert Kennedy.

All the old, natural leftist allegiances were strained, if not completely severed. The average working-class man and woman, the dues-paying union members, had little patience with the hippies or the protestors of the civil rights and antiwar movements. They tended overwhelmingly to see the student demonstrators as coddled children of privilege and/or freaks.

Richard J. Daley, the Chicago mayor who unleashed the furor of the Chicago police— and, it seemed, a huge, outraged block of the populace—on the protestors at the 1968 Democratic convention, was himself a blue-collar Democrat who reviled the hippies and supported the war.

The most powerful political figures of the time—in both parties—represented one of the most awkward, befuddled, charmless, and unphotogenic rogues' galleries in modern American history. The network television anchors were, almost to a man (and they were all, of course, men), older, serious, professorial rather than avuncular. They would have looked right at home at the time in any boardroom, bank, law firm, laboratory, hospital, or other traditional bastion of older, serious white men.

Not everything changed in 1968: bartender and customers at Esslinger's in St. Paul, Minnesota.

Why 1968 rather than, say, 1967 (the Summer of Love) or 1969 (the summer of Woodstock and Altamont, the former, notably, held on a farm, the latter, on a racetrack)?

And the answer, I hope, is in this book somewhere. We are now so far removed from the events of 1968 that even for many people who were alive and fully conscious at the time, all the craziness and passion and unrest of that period is often just lumped together as "the sixties."

But 1968 was unquestionably a remarkable year, even by the standards of the sixties, and in so many ways a pivotal year in the history of the country, and the world.

It was a crucial election year, a particularly bleak year in the Vietnam War, a war that seemed to be spiraling further out of control by the month, its goals and shape and scope constantly shifting, the possibilities and definitions of victory ever more elusive, distressing, and catastrophic. It was a year of wrenching political violence and unrest, both in America and abroad. The country was marked by spectacular divisiveness, between young and old, rich and poor, black and white, North and South, small towns and big cities. It was a year of unprecedented prosperity, at least for the booming white middle class, that masked the largely invisible poverty of the inner cities and rural South. The colleges were full of the children of the post–World War II generation, and these kids had, for the most part, grown up in a world that was radically different from the one that had shaped the ambitions and insecurities of their parents.

It was a year of contrasts and contradictions. There was a generation gap, but there were also gaps everywhere you looked. Blacks and other minorities and women still faced limited prospects in 1968. We still lived in a culture and a society that was shaped and ruled by white men, and there were everywhere stubborn remnants of 1950s America and the paranoia of the Cold War, which the year's events would only rekindle. It was a year of countless acts of principled courage, but also a year of pervasive fear and confusion. Many of the events of 1968 were a direct challenge to the core principles of the so-called Greatest Generation. Every new affront to their values was, after all, an example of the sort of freedoms they had fought for.

What, really, did it mean to live in a free and open society? Where did you draw the line at anarchy?

Internationally, as well as in America, there may have never been a time when the definition of freedom was so relative and nuanced and shape shifting. 1968 brought plenty of examples from elsewhere in the world of the consequences of severe repression. Americans not too distracted by the war in Vietnam and the mounting chaos in their own country could look to Prague or Warsaw or Mexico City or Nigeria or even Paris for evidence of the very real and serious consequences of both personal politics and government action. That they didn't really have to is a statement,

Antiwar protestors, including a young girl handing out literature, in Madison, Wisconsin.

surely, about how chaotic and tenuous the American political and cultural landscape was at the time. We had soldiers in the streets of American cities beating and arresting demonstrators. Open revolt broke out on so many fronts and over so many fundamental issues that the average citizen could barely digest the daily news, which was not even then so thoroughly indigestible as it is now.

1968 was a year that began with violence and confusion, continued to produce violence and confusion in shattering waves, and eventually ended in an untenable stalemate: with a political coronation that seemed to entirely disregard the passion and tumult of the eleven months that preceded it, and then, just as the year drew to a close, with a snapshot of a sort of holistic futurism sent from space and accompanied by a reading from the book of Genesis.

It was a year of mixed messages—many of them delivered with power and passion; others, not so much—and a great divide that has arguably shown few signs of narrowing in the intervening years. Much of the chaos of 1968 was delivered to huge, largely disengaged swaths of the population by the relatively new medium of television, but in such a raw and novel form—TV news was of course not then as slickly produced, edited, and packaged as it is today—the fervor must have looked to many Americans like so much exotic chaos and distressing anarchy.

Is it not possible that even then television had the power to however inadvertently present the various movements of 1968—the civil rights and antiwar demonstrations, the antics of the counterculture, and the emergent voices for Black Power and women's rights—as distant but massing threats to conventional American values and a hard-won prosperity?

In the places where such movements did not yet have a real presence or foothold—and that would have been an enormous territory at the time—all the provocations of 1968 must have been terribly confusing and even terrifying. Was dissent and disorder the future of America? How long could small-town and rural America—in the Midwest, the West, the Rust Belt, and the South—hope to hold its ground and protect its children and its institutions from such wholesale rejection, anger, and nonconformity?

Family farmers survey their autumn bounty at a farmers' market in St. Paul, Minnesota.

TELEVISION WAS PERHAPS in its golden age in terms of influencing public perceptions and opinions, but that, of course, was precisely because it was both something of a novelty and a media monopoly. Many homes subscribed to a local newspaper, and middle- and upper-class families might have received one of a handful of the truly influential and pervasive news magazines—*Life, Look, Time;* even the titles were freighted with significance for an age of "consciousness raising"—but for the first time in history the evening news on the three major networks provided a vital and almost instantaneous glimpse into what was happening elsewhere in the country and the world. Satellite technology and videotape were revolutionizing the speed at which images and information could be delivered to living rooms all over America, and the constant battle for breaking news, combined with the strict, old-school journalism ethos of the men who delivered that news, meant that in that critical time in both the history of the country and the medium, Americans in front of their television sets were receiving remarkably stark and objective versions of the stories of the day. The evening newscasts grew in stature and influence throughout the sixties and early seventies, but 1968 was decidedly the watershed year for television journalism.

There was for sure lots and lots of nifty *stuff* in 1968, perhaps more nifty stuff than ever before—it was a fine time to be a daydreaming child with the J.C. Penney or Sears Christmas catalog in your hands—but there for damn sure weren't so many confounding gizmos. The gee-whizery was less complicated and at the same time seemed somehow more creative. Even a rotary phone or a phonograph still strikes me as more miracle than any reasonable person has any right to expect from this world.

That so much happened in 1968, and on such a large scale and in so many far-flung places—without cell phones, e-mail, Facebook, or Twitter—is one of the real marvels of the year. How the hell did people communicate? Phones were still stationary, and relatively bulky, but they were effective. And people still sent stuff through the mail. The media—television, radio, and print—was all the browser anyone had, yet has there ever been a time when the world felt more truly like a worldwide web (a metaphor that would be driven home by those first photos of Earth sent back from space by *Apollo 8*)?

Even with the advances in satellite technology and videotape, very little news was immediate. Still, word did travel faster than it ever had. Students all over the world could follow what was happening elsewhere through the evening news, transistor radios, and the daily papers. Social networking meant actually getting out into the world and talking to people and sharing ideas and energy face to face. The young activists were a peripatetic bunch; they traveled to the South, traveled abroad, held meetings and organized in towns and cities all over the world. And then they took what they learned and heard and returned home and went to work.

The mimeograph machine had its last

heyday, and the art of silk screen posters flourished and supported the messages of political and activist movements. Immediately iconic and beautiful images and messages appeared on walls and telephone poles around the globe.

THERE WAS ALSO A CONFLUENCE of synergistic cultural touchstones and guidebooks and exemplars for impressionable, curious, or disaffected young people—Herbert Marcuse, Marshall McLuhan, Franz Fanon, Che Guevara, Mao, Gandhi, Malcolm X, Eldridge Cleaver's *Soul on Ice,* the Cuban Revolution, Eastern religion, the speeches of Martin Luther King and the civil disobedience primer provided by his Southern Christian Leadership Conference, Mario Savio, Betty Friedan's *The Feminine Mystique,* Carlos Castaneda, Daniel Berrigan, Allen Ginsberg, Noam Chomsky, and

scores of activist journalists, pamphleteers, and provocateurs—that provided philosophical and strategic groundwork (sometimes pie in the sky, sometimes practical) for budding dissenters. Combine all that fuel with the sudden proliferation of so much dissent—the war, civil rights, economic inequality, campus politics, sexual repression, women's rights, the conformity of the Eisenhower fifties—and you had both a social and cultural tinderbox and the means and motives to ignite it.

I FEEL LIKE I SHOULD be better able to understand the hippies and the Yippies and the civil rights and student demonstrators of 1968, yet I often wonder if there has been anything in my life, or in the lives of subsequent generations, that has even come close to inspiring that sort of principled and courageous action. It is, I know, shameful that at

Comedian Dick Gregory, best known for his comedy albums and political stance in the civil rights movement, ran for president on the Peace and Freedom Party ticket.

least from a personal standpoint there has not, and I recognize that there surely should have been *something*. Yet the principled fringe on both sides of the political divide seems to have shrunk in the intervening decades, and the principled middle is, I believe, large but largely decorous to a fault, and perhaps even a bit timorous.

What would happen, though, if the military draft were reinstituted? Or if some large and principled demonstration of the principled middle was routed by police and National Guard troops? What would happen if one of our national leaders were to be assassinated? Is there anyone left in whom so much hope and faith has been invested that their murder would set off massive upheaval in cities all over the country? Granted, we still have relatively small and civil demonstrations in America, and the occasional minor riots, usually inspired by the killings of citizens (minorities, usually) by police officers (mostly in inner cities), but these events tend to be blips in the cable news cycle and don't tend to lead to lasting or influential movements.

So what, I wonder, would it take in twenty-first-century America to inspire the sorts of huge and widespread expressions of outrage and disapproval that we saw in 1968?

Perhaps, and perhaps inevitably, the birth of the television generation and the influence of the medium, coupled with the economic prosperity of 1968, had an influence that went well beyond bringing the events of that historic year into people's homes with such immediacy. In the long term, the explosion of mass advertising, consumer culture, and unprecedented middle-class buying power likely did more to thwart the various radical propositions being floated by a generation of dissidents.

Television's influence on the culture of dissent and the ease with which it allowed the propagation of that culture's messages on a global scale was without question significant in the context of the time, but in the end all those hours the children of 1968 spent in front of the television ultimately reinforced an older version of the American Dream—a covetous, aspirational means to contentment, through stable, well-paying jobs, education, and buying power—and it is difficult not to conclude that that old version has had a more lasting and unfortunate influence.

Children watching television in a Minneapolis, Minnesota, housing development.

You don't have to look very hard or very far to find, even in the midst of so much almost-revolutionary rhetoric and demonstration, countless powerful examples of propaganda for the upwardly mobile status quo. The country, after all, rode out the turmoil of 1968 and sent Richard Nixon to the White House. But even Nixon's ignominious fall from power could not provide anything but short-lived validation for a generation of sixties radicals. The Vietnam War would outlive even Nixon, and in 1980 America would deliver the final body blow to the ideals of the true believers of 1968 by awarding the presidency—in a historic landslide—to Ronald Reagan, the California governor who was one of the counterculture's most reviled bugbears.

The war and the shattering violence and the constant turmoil on the television dominated virtually my entire childhood and certainly my formative years—I turned seven in 1968 and would be a teenager by the time it all played out and plunged into the malaise of the late seventies. When people fret about television violence today they are largely talking about commodified violence, violence packaged as programming. In 1968 the news represented all the reality TV America needed, and it didn't shy away from violence.

I've often wondered what effect that period, and that unfiltered exposure to the unvarnished reality of the world, had on people of my generation. A kid in 1968 could go to the doctor's office and see photos of dead soldiers, starving children, and demonstrators clashing with baton-wielding police

officers in the pages of *Life* magazine. It's hard, frankly, not to be puzzled. Did all that violence and upheaval somehow drive the country back into a pre-JFK Cold War comfort zone of conformity?

Certainly the edgier members of my generation appropriated the superficial trappings of the sixties counterculture, or at least the more decadent and permissive liberties, but the culture of my adolescence seemed shallow, disaffected but also disengaged, a vacuum that produced punk rock and Margaret Thatcher and Ronald Reagan, who easily won the presidency in the first election in which I was eligible to vote.

That didn't make sense to me at the time, and now, having spent months revisiting and reliving the events of 1968, it makes even less sense to me.

What really happened in 1968? What were the lessons and legacies of that year? Certainly from the vantage of the subsequent decades you can see that there have been incremental changes and victories on many of 1968's most active fronts, but few of them seem substantial enough that they mustn't still be regarded as qualified, at the very least by the people still engaged in fighting those battles at the grassroots level.

If anything, the America of today faces many of the same basic challenges that it spent 1968 wrestling with: a protracted war (or wars), law and order, the threat of violence on both the national and international fronts, rampant consumerism coupled with growing economic disparity, the moldering of inner cities and de facto segregation, an angry and vocal and mobilized segment of the populace, and violent, revolutionary upheaval in cities around the globe. Add to that the saturation of virtually unregulated media, the broad reach (and ripe opportunities for misinformation and overheated rhetoric) provided by the Internet and social media, and the unprecedented influence of a bloated and often appallingly uncredentialed class of partisan pundits, and it seems inevitable that political activism—such as it is—would have become a more sedentary activity, equal parts parlor game, spectator sport, and entertainment.

Yet there is still no getting around the reality that in 2011 in America the loudest and most active heirs to the political dissent of 1968 are largely dedicated to overhauling and undermining the lasting contributions of the generation of Martin Luther King, Robert Kennedy, Stokely Carmichael, Jerry Rubin, Betty Friedan, and Cesar Chavez.

On August 9, 1974, following Richard Nixon's resignation from the presidency, Gerald Ford proclaimed, "The long national nightmare is over." It was at the time an explicit reference to the Watergate scandal and Nixon's resignation, but by the end of 1968 it seemed very much like the long national nightmare was just getting started in earnest.

1969 brought the nostalgic mess of Woodstock, the deadly anarchy of Altamont, and the Manson family murders. Two of the most passionate and politicized songs of the era, Sly and the Family Stone's "There's a Riot Goin' On" and Marvin Gaye's "What's Going On"—both of which seem like pure products of 1968—were released in 1971.

The official end of the Vietnam War wouldn't come until January of 1973; the last troops were supposedly withdrawn in March of that year, yet the fall of Saigon, the evacuation of the American embassy, and the death of the last American soldier didn't take place until the end of April in 1975, seven years after the peak of the protest movements against the war. The war outlasted Nixon,

Lance Corporal Ernest Delgado was photographed at Khe Sanh in March of 1968. By the end of the year, Delgado's tour had ended, and the Americans had abandoned the military base.

and five years after the fall of Saigon the 1968 generation suffered perhaps its final, ironic knockout blow when Ronald Reagan, the anti-hippie, law-and-order governor of California during that tumultuous and idealistic year, was elected president in one of the biggest landslides in American political history.

The Equal Rights Amendment, originally introduced in 1923, didn't pass both houses of Congress until 1972 and has still not been ratified on the federal level. On the state level, fifteen states have still not gotten around to ratifying the ERA.

Sexism is still with us. Bigotry in its myriad forms is still with us. States' rights are still alive and well, and have recently been revived by all sorts of zealots who would like to roll back a great deal of the progress the zealots of 1968 fought for.

We are still slouching toward Bethlehem, but the devastating couplet of Yeats' "Second Coming"—"The best lack all conviction and the worst are full of passionate intensity"—which was so completely turned on its head in 1968, has been brought back into its original, despairing alignment and often seems to ring more true than ever today.

The country has been embroiled in lingering and costly wars that have brought frequent comparisons to Vietnam. We have a stagnant economy, a shrinking middle class, and a widening gap between the rich and poor. Gas prices are at record levels. The Internet and telecommunications and global culture have created an ersatz sense of community, even as they have also made possible all sorts

of spirited and often effective political demonstrations in the Middle East and North Africa. Whether these realities and resources will become effective motivators and tools to support real organization and activism for a generation of younger Americans is still very much up in the air.

In the United States, street demonstrations have been replaced by star-studded benefit concerts and fundraising efforts, the metaphorical and literal web of the Internet, and the ceaseless squall from the Babel of punditry. It is easier than ever to consume and at least partially digest what is happening in the country from the safe refuge of one's home or desk. Access to so much news and information from every imaginable slant creates the illusion—or delusion—that we are sufficiently engaged even if we have nothing more than an opinion. Here, perhaps, is a relevant question: Did the dissent—for the most part squelched and unrewarded—of 1968 and the tumultuous years preceding and following it represent the defeat of such spirited and large-scale protest in this country? Did the hard lessons and defeats of those years turn that generation—and subsequent generations—inward? Did it make them cynical or disenchanted with their version of the American Dream?

CONVERSATIONS I HAD in the course of researching and writing this book made it apparent that the average person of my generation has only a vague historical grasp of that year. It was a remarkable and disturbing time, but it was also a long time ago. Examining it in excruciating detail from the vantage of a remarkable and disturbing time early in the twenty-first century raises all sorts of questions, the same sorts of questions that were being asked with great passion and desperate curiosity forty-three years ago, many of which, it seems, still have no satisfactory answers.

What still seems so startling about that year and that time is precisely the extent to which so many big questions *were* being asked, were being publicly and urgently asked by large numbers of people all over the world, and were being debated and violently contested by people from all walks of life; this was not idle dorm room or dinner table conversation, although some of that was certainly going on as well. The big questions were not only being asked; the people asking them were demanding answers. They wanted explanations. They wanted solutions. They wanted change. This was the generation that threw out *Robert's Rules of Order.*

The askers of questions in 1968 wanted a purified and pliable democracy, something like the Walt Whitman version. They had no choice but to be organized, aggressive, and demonstrative, to ask their questions in the only place where they could be heard: The streets. The campuses. The pulpits and the podiums. Out in the world.

They asked their questions, and if their questions did not ultimately receive satisfactory answers from the people to whom they were directed, they kept asking them anyway, and some of them found their own answers along the way, and those answers shaped their lives. And that, perhaps, is the true lasting legacy of 1968.

ESSAY ON SOURCES

1968 HAS BEEN the subject of several books, and there is of course an extensive literature on the 1960s more generally. A short list follows; these books have been consulted in assembling the text as a whole and are cited more specifically where appropriate.

1968

Ali, Tariq, and Susan Watkins. *1968: Marching in the Streets*. New York: Free Press, 1998.

The Associated Press. *The World in 1968: History as We Lived It*. Racine, WI: Western Publishing Company, 1969.

Caute, David. *The Year of the Barricades: A Journey through 1968*. New York: Harper and Row, 1988.

Fraser, Ronald, ed. *1968: A Student Revolution in Revolt: An International Oral History*. New York: Pantheon, 1988.

Kaiser, Charles. *1968 in America: Music, Politics, Chaos, Counterculture, and the Shaping of a Generation*. New York: Grove Press, 1997.

Kaufman, Michael. *1968*. New York: Macmillan, 2009.

Kurlansky, Mark. *1968: The Year that Rocked the World*. New York: Random House, 2004.

Magnum Photos. *1968 Magnum Throughout the World*. Paris: Hazan, 1998.

Witcover, Jules. *The Year the Dream Died: Revisiting 1968 in America*. New York: Warner Books, 1997.

Introduction

It would be impossible to reference the entire body of work on the sixties. Books we found particularly useful include *The Sixties: From Memory to History* (Chapel Hill: University of North Carolina Press, 1994), an excellent collection of essays by leading historians, edited by David Farber, and Gerard DeGroot's *The Sixties Unplugged: A Kaleidoscopic History of a Disorderly Decade* (Cambridge, MA: Harvard University Press, 2008), a stimulating, unruly, and anti-nostalgic history. Mike Wallace and other student activists, including Mario Savio and Mark Rudd, were interviewed by the Columbia University Center for Oral History's Student Movements of the 1960s Project in the mid-1980s.

January

Quotations from Charles Branham, Tim O'Brien, and Sara Evans come from interviews conducted by Brian Horrigan for The 1968 Exhibit. The phrase "living-room war" comes from Michael J. Arlen, television critic for The *New Yorker,* who coined it in a 1966 column. This piece and many others about television and politics in the late 1960s are available in Arlen's book, *Living-Room War* (New York: Viking Press, 1969).

The literature on Vietnam is intimidating in its vastness and contentiousness. Again, works that we found particularly helpful in shaping this book include Stanley Karnow's *Vietnam: A History* (New York: Viking, 1983), the standard history, and still one of the best; while *America and the Vietnam War* (New York: Routledge, 2010), edited by Andrew Wiest, Mary Kathryn Barbier, and Glenn Robins, is a fine new collection of scholarly essays. Lawrence M. Baskir and William A. Strauss's *Chance and Circumstance: The Draft, the War, and the Vietnam Generation* (New York: Knopf, 1978) provides an in-depth study on the demographics of the U.S. military during the war.

February

Quotations from Vietnam War officials come from William G. Effros's *Quotations: Vietnam: 1945–1970* (New York: Random House, 1970); while quotations from Patrick Edmondson and Vietnam veterans Charles Carlson, Will Smith, and Gilbert de la O are drawn from a series of oral histories conducted by Brian Horrigan and Douglas Bekke for The 1968 Exhibit. Tim O'Brien is the author of several books that draw on his army experiences in Vietnam, including the novel *The Things They Carried* (New York: Houghton Mifflin, 1990) and a memoir, *If I Die in a Combat Zone, Box Me up and Ship Me Home* (New York: Delacorte, 1973).

Moving Image

Mark Harris's *Pictures at a Revolution: Five Movies and the Birth of the New Hollywood* (New York: Penguin, 2008) discusses the changing milieu of Hollywood through the lens of the five 1967 movies competing for Best Picture at the Academy Awards held in April 1968. *Easy Riders, Raging Bulls: How the Sex-Drugs-and-Rock 'N' Roll Generation Saved Hollywood* (New York: Simon & Schuster, 1999), by Peter Biskind, tells the story of the next decade of New Hollywood. Sixties television has been the subject of several books: for an academic take, Aniko Bodroghkozy's *Groove Tube: Sixties Television and the Youth Rebellion* (Durham, NC: Duke University Press, 2001) is quite accessible and covers *Julia* and the Smothers Brothers in depth. Steven Stark's *Glued to the Set: The 60 Television Shows and Events That Made Us Who We Are Today* (New York: Free Press, 1997) covers a wider swath of history but makes insightful comments about the era, and the year, in particular.

March

SDS leader (and media scholar) Todd Gitlin's *The Sixties: Years of Hope, Days of Rage* (New York: Bantam Books, 1987) is a classic account, particularly of campus unrest during this period. Quotations from Grace LeClair are taken from her oral history interview with Brian Horrigan; Mark Rudd's quotation can be found in Kurlansky, as can Kurlansky's insight about the changing perception of the university in American life. Coverage of "The LeClair Affair" was extensive in the *New York Times;* the article called "The Arrangement," by William A. McWhirter, was published in *Life,* May 31, 1968. Beth Bailey also covers the story, and many of the other changes in American discourse around sexuality in the 1960s, in her book *Sex in the Heartland* (Cambridge, MA: Harvard University Press, 2002).

Nicholas von Hoffman's *We Are the People Our Parents Warned Us Against,* published in 1968, is a compelling document of San Francisco's counterculture. Many people who volunteered or worked on the McCarthy campaign wrote about their activities, including Jeremy Larner in *Nobody Knows: Reflections on the McCarthy Campaign of 1968* (New York: Macmillan, 1969) and Arthur Herzog in *McCarthy for President* (New York: Viking, 1970). Witcover's *The Year the Dream Died* is an excellent overall account of American politics that year, with special emphasis on the McCarthy and Kennedy campaigns.

April

King's life and actions have been extensively documented, perhaps most notably by Taylor Branch in his *America in the King Years* series; the book *At Canaan's Edge: America in the King Years, 1965–1968* (New York: Simon & Schuster, 2006) covers the last years of King's life. King's speeches quoted here can be found in James Melvin Washington's edited collection *A Testament of Hope: The Essential Writings and Speeches of Martin Luther King* (New York: HarperCollins, 1991). American RadioWorks's "King's Last March" provided much of the background on King's later organizing efforts, as did Michael Eric Dyson's *April 4, 1968: Martin Luther King, Jr.'s Death and How it Changed America* (New York: Basic Civitas, 2008). Rebecca Burns's *Burial for a King: Martin Luther King Jr.'s Funeral and the Week that Transformed Atlanta and Rocked the Nation* (New York: Simon & Schuster, 2011) provides much more detail about the funeral itself, while Hampton Sides's *Hellhound on His Trail: The Stalking of Martin Luther King Jr. and the International Hunt for His Assassin* (New York: Doubleday, 2010) is a lightly fictionalized account of James Earl Ray's actions and King's last days. Quotations from Brenda Banks and Carole Merritt come from oral history interviews with Brian Horrigan; Banks is former deputy director of the Georgia State Archives; Merritt and Banks worked together to organize and digitize the Martin Luther King Jr. papers at Morehouse College. James Brown's autobiography, *James Brown: The Godfather of Soul* (with Bruce Tucker; New York: Macmillan, 1986), provides some insight into his actions in 1968.

May

Many of the quotations from participants in the Poor People's Campaign, including Tilly Walker's (from an interview with PPC staff Kay Shannon) are taken from Gordon Keith Mantler's (unpublished) PhD dissertation, "Black, Brown, and Poor: Martin Luther King Jr., the Poor People's Campaign, and Its Legacies" (Duke University, 2008). Quotations from Ralph Abernathy and participation figures come from the Associated Press's *The World in 1968: History as We Lived It*. A *Weekend America* story on Resurrection City also provided insight and firsthand accounts of life in the tent city and is available at http://weekendamerica.publicradio.org/display/web/2008/05/08/1968_resurrection/.

June

Paul Fusco's funeral train photographs were published with essays by Evan Thomas and Norman Mailer in *RFK Funeral Train* (New York: Umbrage Editions, 2001). Bill Eppridge, who took the famous photograph of Kennedy's assassination in this chapter, also photographed from the moving funeral train. He recounts his experiences in *A Time It Was: Bobby Kennedy in the Sixties* (New York: Abrams, 2008). Evan Thomas and Arthur Schlesinger have both published respected biographies of Kennedy as well: *Robert Kennedy: His Life* (New York: Simon & Schuster, 2000) and *Robert Kennedy and His Times* (New York: Ballantine Books, 1978), respectively. Thurston Clarke's *The Last Campaign: Robert Kennedy and 82 Days that Changed America* (New York: Henry Holt and Company, 2008) is a more recent history of Kennedy's presidential campaign and its effects.

Music

J. Marks's *Rock and Other Four-Letter Words* (New York: Bantam, 1968) features photographs by a pre-McCartney Linda Eastman and is an excellent primary source. The Rock and Roll Hall of Fame Museum published a retrospective of the period as well: *I Want to Take You Higher: The Psychedelic Era, 1965–1969* (San Francisco, CA: Chronicle Books, 1997). *Motown: Music, Money, Sex, and Power* (New York: Random House, 2005), by Gerald Posner, provides a meticulously researched look at Berry Gordy and his record label.

July

Jon Erikson's photographs are featured in The 1968 Exhibit; they were published with Robert Coles's prose in *The Middle Americans: Proud and Uncertain* (New York: Little, Brown, 1971). Many authors have traced the rise of contemporary conservatism to 1968. Dan Carter's *The Politics of Rage: George Wallace, the Origins of the New Conservatism, and the Transformation of American Politics* (New York: Simon & Schuster, 1995) and Lisa McGirr's *Suburban Warriors: The Origins of the New American Right* (Princeton, NJ: Princeton University Press, 2001) are particularly valuable.

August

Norman Mailer's *Miami and the Siege of Chicago* (1968) began as an assignment for *Harper's* magazine. It was republished by New York Review Books Classics in 2008. Gitlin's *Years of Hope, Days of Rage* provides a different point of view on Chicago. Twenty years after the events, historian David Farber chronicled them in his *Chicago '68* (Chicago: University of Chicago Press, 1988). For more information on Alexander Dubcek and the Prague Spring, *Prague's 200 Days*, published in 1969 by Harry Schwartz, is a good place to start. You can find excerpts from the 1968 Action Program online at http://personal.ashland.edu/~jmoser1/action program.htm, and a valuable timeline of events compiled by Radio Free Europe at http://www.rferl.org/content/article/1089303.html.

September

Sara Evans, professor emerita of women's and gender studies at the University of Minnesota, is one of her generation's most prominent chroniclers of second-wave feminism; her book *Personal Politics: The Roots of Women's Liberation in the Civil Rights Movements and the New Left* (New York: Vintage, 1979) begins the tale, and her more recent *Tidal Wave: How Women Changed America at Century's End* (New York: Free Press, 2004) continues it. She was interviewed by Brian Horrigan on March 28, 2011, for The 1968 Exhibit. Pat Montandon's *How to Be a Party Girl* (New York: McGraw-Hill, 1968) provides a window into an empowered, girlish femininity that draws on Helen Gurley Brown's *Sex and the Single Girl,* which had been providing urban women with professional and personal advice since 1962. Elaine Tyler May's *America and the Pill: A History of Promise, Peril, and Liberation* (New York: Basic Books, 2010) provides a history of the sexual revolution, as does WGBH/American Experience's *The Pill* (available on DVD; more information at http://www.pbs.org/wgbh/amex/pill). Ali and Watkins's book provides an in-depth account of the Miss America protest, drawing on Robin Morgan's memoir, *Going Too Far: The Personal Chronicle of a Feminist* (New York: Random House, 1978). New York Radical Women's "No More Miss America" manifesto can be read in full online at http://www.feministezine.com/feminist/modern/No-More-Ms-America.html.

October

Peniel E. Joseph's edited volume *The Black Power Movement: Rethinking the Civil Rights–Black Power Era* (New York: Routledge, 2006) contains an array of scholarly perspectives on SNCC, the Panthers, black feminism, and other aspects of this pivotal era. Many activists, including Elaine Brown (*A Taste of Power: A Black Woman's Story* [New York: Pantheon Books, 1992]), have written valuable memoirs about their work, and Eldridge Cleaver's *Soul on Ice,* published in 1968, is an invaluable primary and secondary source. Some of the reflections on the 1968 Olympics come from Richard Hoffer's *Something in the Air: American Passion and Defiance in the 1968 Mexico City Olympics* (New York: Free Press, 2009). Gwen Patton's essay can be found in *Hands on the Freedom Plow: Personal Accounts by Women in SNCC* (Urbana: University of Illinois Press, 2010).

For more on the Brown Berets and the Chicano Civil Rights Movement, *Chicano!: The History of the Mexican American Civil Rights Movement,* by Arturo Rosales (Houston, TX: Arte Publico Press, 1996), is a thorough history of Mexican American presence and activism in the twentieth-century United States. Carlos Muñoz's *Youth, Identity, Power: The Chicano Movement* (New York: Verso, 1989) is a more scholarly telling that focuses on the 1960s and 1970s. "A Brief History of the American Indian Movement" can be found at http://www.aimove ment.org/ggc/history.html. Ward Churchill and Jim Vanderwall's *Agents of Repression* ties together AIM and the Panthers' decades-long struggle against repression, exposing the threat the U.S. government felt these organizations posed. Kurlansky provides a valuable overview of the events of the summer and fall of 1968 in Mexico City; Elena Poniatowska's *Massacre in Mexico* (Columbia: University of Missouri Press, 1975) is an in-depth oral history. More information on new sources, including interviews with protestors and government footage of the massacre, is available through NPR's *Radio Diaries* installment on the Tlatelolco massacre (listen at http://radiodiaries.org) and George Washington University's National Security Archives Mexico Project (http://www.gwu.edu/~nsarchiv/mexico/).

November

Lewis Chester, Godfrey Hodgson, and Bruce Page juicily characterize the election season in their *An American Melodrama: The Presidential Campaign of 1968* (New York: Viking, 1969). Witcover's book is also particularly focused on that year's presidential race and personalities. Rick Perlstein's *Nixonland: The Rise of a President and the Fracturing of America* (New York: Scribner, 2008) is a comprehensive account of Nixon's rise to power and its consequences for American politics.

Fashion, Design, Consumerism

Much of this chapter (and the other interludes as well) is drawn from Brian Horrigan's *Covering 1968* blog; the full archives are available at http://www. the1968exhibit.org/covering-1968. Thomas Frank's *Conquest of Cool: Business Culture, Counterculture, and the Rise of Hip Consumerism* (Chicago: University of Chicago Press, 1998) informs the analysis here. Philippe Garner wrote a lovely Taschen book, *Sixties Design,* with a wide array of striking period images (Cologne: Taschen, 2003).

December

Several books have been written about NASA in the 1960s, particularly the Apollo program. Additionally, NASA has conducted a series of oral history interviews about Apollo and other projects, including an audio documentary about *Apollo 8,* all available at http://www.jsc.nasa.gov/history/ oral_histories/oral_histories.htm. Richard Orloff and David Harland's *Apollo: The Definitive Sourcebook* (New York: Springer, 2006) was particularly useful in assembling this chapter. *A Man on the Moon: The Voyages of the Apollo Astronauts,* by Andrew Chaikin and Tom Hanks (New York: Penguin, 2007), provides more information on the men who went to the moon.

CONTRIBUTORS AND ACKNOWLEGMENTS

CONTRIBUTORS

Brian Horrigan (who turned eighteen in 1968) has been an exhibit curator at the Minnesota Historical Society since 1990. Educated at the University of Chicago and the University of California—Berkeley, he has also developed exhibits for the Smithsonian Institution, the National Park Service, the U.S. Navy, and, in the 1980s, for cultural exchange programs between the United States and the former U.S.S.R.

Brad Zellar is an award-winning journalist, writer, and editor and the author of *Suburban World: The Norling Photographs*. His work has appeared in various publications and anthologies. His most recent books are *Conductors of the Moving World* and *House of Coates*, a collaboration with Lester B. Morrison.

Elizabeth Ault is a PhD candidate in the Department of American Studies at the University of Minnesota—Twin Cities. Her dissertation, "Take Responsibility for Your *Good Times*: Black Sitcoms, Citizenship, and the Reinvention of Government 1972—1984," is focused on events that occurred in the wake of 1968. A graduate of Brown University, she is a child of children of the sixties.

Maggie Nancarrow is a research assistant on The 1968 Exhibit. A graduate in history and religion from Hamline University, she also is a marker artist and works for building cross-cultural community. She is currently pursuing a master of divinity at the University of Chicago.

John Vanek is currently pursuing a PhD in history at the University of Delaware. He served as a primary contributor to a number of music-related projects for The 1968 Exhibit.

ACKNOWLEDGMENTS

The 1968 Exhibit was produced by the Minnesota Historical Society in partnership with the Atlanta History Center, the Chicago History Museum, and the Oakland Museum of California. We are grateful to the staffs of all of our partner institutions and to our project's numerous scholarly advisors. Additionally, we'd like to thank those who shared their stories of 1968 through participating in oral history interviews or posting on the project website. The Minnesota Historical Society also gratefully acknowledges the support of the National Endowment for the Humanities, which awarded the society an Exhibit Planning Grant in 2009 and a Chairman's Special Award for Exhibit Implementation in 2010; and the Institute of Museum and Library Services, which awarded the society a "Museums for America" grant in 2009. The 1968 Exhibit also received a "We the People" project designation from the National Endowment for the Humanities for its contribution to the study of American culture.

As with any major museum undertaking, The 1968 Exhibit involved the mobilization of huge armies of talented people, too many to enumerate here. In addition to all of the members of the extraordinary team at the Minnesota Historical Society that produced the exhibit, I would like to thank by name a group that often goes overlooked: the researchers, interns, and design assistants—some of them volunteers and all of them *way* too young to remember 1968—who worked on the project over the course of nearly four years: Katie Bates, Jesse Cogswell, Melissa Gagner, Ned Hurley, Becki Iverson, Adam K. Jones, Milo Mietzner, Jesada Moua, Maggie Nancarrow, Jenny Parker, Mark Schultz, Sean Traynor, and John Vanek. —B.H.

I'd like to thank Geoff Garton, Peter Schilling, Andy Sturdevant, and Deborah Rybak for their help with brainstorming and source materials, as well as general encouragement. And I am hugely indebted especially to Elizabeth Ault and Pam McClanahan of the Minnesota Historical Society for assistance (and patience) above and beyond the call of duty. —B.Z.

Many thanks to everyone who helped put this book together—Minnesota Historical Society staff are not only terrific at their jobs; they're gracious, too. In exhibits and collections, Brian Horrigan, Rich Rummel, Maggie Nancarrow, Earl Gutnik, Ann Frisina, Jason Onerheim, and Nicole Delfino Jansen helped this novice learn the ropes. The MHS Press team provided a crash course in publishing, and Pam McClanahan was the dynamic force behind it. Thanks to her and Shannon Pennefeather, in particular, for time traveling back to 1968 with me, Brad, and Brian over these months. Thanks also to Mike Blank, Mei-Ling Anderson, and Nancy Clayton Ault for their insights on (respectively) baseball, Paris, and the pleasures of being a square. —E.A.

IMAGE CREDITS

The 1968 Exhibit
    Page 17 (Brady Willette)
Guy Anhorn
    Pages 29, 30 (bottom)
Kenan Research Center at the Atlanta History Center
    Pages 97 (bottom: Bill Wilson), 134 (right)
Baltimore County Public Library
    Page 65 (bottom left)
Beinecke Rare Book and Manuscript Library, Yale University
    Page 70
Bettman/CORBIS
    Page 122
The California State University, Los Angeles, John F. Kennedy Memorial Library, The Gloria Arellanes Papers
    Page 124 (top and bottom)
Chicago History Museum
    Pages 57 (neg. iCHi-62895), 74 (neg. iCHi-62719), 76 (bottom: neg. iCHi-62720), 79 (neg. iCHi-62718), 98 (top: neg. iChi-62878)—all Declan Haun; pages 99 (neg. iCHi-62713) and 100 (bottom left: neg. iCHi-62716)—both Charles Roland; bottom right; page 100 (neg. iCHi-37012)
The Comisar Collection, Inc.
    Pages 37, 38 (top and bottom), 128 (right)—all Jason Onerheim
Alix Kates Shulman Papers, Rare Book, Manuscript, and Special Collections Library, Duke University, Durham, North Carolina
    Pages 106 (top), 116

Ebenezer Baptist Church
    Pages 61 (*Atlanta Inquirer*), 63 (bottom)
Evan Freed
    Page 75
George Mason University Libraries, Special Collections & Archives
    Pages 66 (Jack Rottier Photograph Collection #C0003); 68 (top and bottom) and 130—all Oliver F. Atkins Photograph Collection #C0036
Getty Images
    Pages 33 (Susan Wood), 34 (Paramount Pictures), 39 (NBC Television), 42 (photo by Ronald L. Haeberle / TIME & LIFE Images), 43 (top: Hulton Archive), 58 and 85 (photos by Tom Copi/Michael Ochs Archives), 77 and 78 (photos by Bill Eppridge/Time Life Pictures), 81 (Fred W. McDarrah), 82 (Elliot Landy/Redferns), 90 (bottom) and 110 (Leonard Burt/Stinger), 93 (Neil Leifer/Sports Illustrated), 107 (CBS), 129 (Walter Iooss)
Earl Gutnik, exhibit designer, Minnesota Historical Society
    Pages 25 (top), 31, 52 (right), 55 (top), 80, 86, 90 (top), 98 (bottom), 138, 139, 140, 141 (bottom)—all photographed by Petronella J. Ytsma; pages 83, 92, 109 (left), 115 (all), 141 (top), 142 (middle)—all photographed by Bill Jolitz
Institute of National Remembrance, Poland
    Page 106 (bottom)
Laura Jones
    Page 67 (bottom)

Library of Congress

Pages 24 (Marion S. Trikosko, U.S. News & World Report), 67 (top right: Warren K. Leffler, U.S. News & World Report), 73 (left), 128 (left: Roger Higgins, New York World-Telegram & Sun)

Lyndon Baines Johnson Library

Pages 15 (left: Kevin Smith); 20 (left) and 54—both Frank Wolfe; 22 (bottom), 43 (bottom), 65 (top), and 131—all Yoichi Okamoto; 28 (Jack Kightlinger); 73 (right: Robert Knudsen), 119 (Mike Geissinger)

Magnum Images

Page 56 (Danny Lyon)

Marcel-lí Perello

Pages 118 (top), 127

Minnesota Historical Society Collections, St. Paul

Pages 18 (Norton & Peel), 26 (top: Petronella J. Ytsma), 44–45, 47, 48 (Eugene Debs Becker), 49 (bottom), 52 (left), 55 (bottom), 60 (Mike Zerby), 76 (top), 91, 100 (top), 102 (Earl Seubert), 108, 109 (right: Minneapolis *Star*), 113, 120 (Minneapolis *Tribune*), 125 (courtesy Dick Bancroft), 135, 149 (3M Company), 150 (Harry Benbrooke Hall), 152, 155; pages 21 (right), 26 (bottom), 49 (top), 103, 111, 132, 146 (bottom), 154—all photographed by Bill Jolitz

NASA/courtesy of nasaimages.org

Pages 144, 146 (top), 147

National Archives

Pages 25 (bottom), 27

National Parks Service

Page 65 (bottom right)

Charles Deering McCormick Library of Special Collections, Northwestern University Library

Pages 101 (all) and 104—all Kaye Miller Collection

Division of Political History, National Museum of American History, Smithsonian Institution

Pages 22 (top), 23 (right), 51, 63 (top), 67 (top left), 70, 97 (top), 126, 134 (left)

SRI International

Page 142 (top right)

Stanford News Service

Pages 14 and 145—both Chuck Painter

United States Air Force

Pages 15 (right), 118 (bottom)

University of Minnesota Libraries and Special Collections

Pages 50, 53 (all)

Harry Ransom Humanities Research Center, University of Texas at Austin

Pages 30 (top) and 157—both © David Duncan Douglas, David Duncan Douglas Archive

University of Wisconsin, Madison

Pages 20 (right), 21 (left), 23 (left), 151

INDEX

The 1968 Exhibit playlist is available for download from iTunes.

1968 movie recommendations are available through Netflix.

Find out more about The 1968 Exhibit, read the *Covering 1968* blog, and share your reflections on the year at http://www.the1968exhibit.org/.